S0-AXX-167

June 22, 1966

To June

with love

Gil & Kay

Happy Birthday

COWBOY AT THE MIKE

COWBOY
AT THE MIKE

CURT GOWDY

WITH AL HIRSHBERG

1966

DOUBLEDAY & COMPANY, INC.
GARDEN CITY, NEW YORK

Library of Congress Catalog Card Number 64-13818
Copyright © 1966 by Curt Gowdy and Al Hirshberg
All Rights Reserved
Printed in the United States of America
First Edition

To Jerre, my wife,
in grateful appreciation
of her help and
understanding.

COWBOY AT THE MIKE

1

No matter how hard I tried I was never able to get rid of an accent so pronounced that whoever hears me knows I couldn't have come from anywhere but the land of the big sky and the wide open spaces. My flat voice sounds just the way a cowboy hat looks. It's as characteristic of my native Wyoming as the clop-clop of antelope hoofs and the splashing of mountain trout and the breathtaking beauty of the Rockies at twilight and the mournful whistle of Union Pacific engines as they roar toward the Continental Divide.

I guess this accent helps me in New England, where I have been broadcasting Boston Red Sox games since 1951, maybe because most of the people who hear my voice don't ever hear anything quite like it except when I'm on the air. Yet I continued to try to get rid of it until perhaps ten years ago when a local boy auditioned to be one of my assistants. I wanted to hire him, but the sponsors and the radio and television brass and everyone else who had anything to do with the broadcasts turned him down cold. They didn't like his Boston accent. Then and there I stopped trying to change my Wyoming one.

I was born in Green River, a small town in the southwestern part of the state, but I grew up in Cheyenne, where my father, a railroad man all his life, became chief dispatcher for the Union Pacific when I was six years old. Cheyenne may sound like the end of nowhere to a lot of people, but it was—and is—a marvelous place for a boy to grow up. We made our own fun, and had plenty of it.

Fishing and hunting and sports were the big things of my life. We kids used to go out and hunt cottontails and jackrabbits right on the edge of town, just a few blocks from my house. A mile or two beyond there were herds of antelope, and if we wanted to play cowboys we didn't have to go that far. Right in town was the famous Cheyenne Frontier Days, the best-known rodeo grounds in the West. Sometimes we'd go over there and ride and rope goats and calves and just bum around. The men in town had calf-roping clubs, and we used to sit and cheer our favorites, as if they were college football teams and we the student bodies.

Wyoming has some of the best trout fishing in the world. There's not much around Cheyenne itself, but within thirty-five or forty miles are little-known, out-of-the-way streams with fish as eager to be caught as fishermen to catch them. Around Laramie, just on the other side of the mountains from Cheyenne, streams and runlets and rivers are jumping with trout. Even when I was little I managed to get over there pretty often.

My dad worked twelve hours a day seven days a week, but sometimes he sneaked off early to take me fly fishing. Other times I'd get a ride with one of the kids in the neighborhood. There was always somebody going somewhere for trout because in that part of Wyoming fishing isn't just a sport—it's a way of life. I can't remember a male from the age of six up around there who wouldn't rather fish than eat.

And to this day I haven't changed. I still love it beyond any other pastime, and have traveled thousands of miles to indulge in it, for fishing is in my blood. One of my greatest thrills was the first time I took my older son, Curt, Jr., back to Wyoming to fish in the streams of my boyhood. They haven't changed either. They've got the same branches, the same ripples, the same turns, the same holes, the same stretches of water that they had in my youth. And the trout bite as enthusiastically today as they did thirty-five years ago.

Wyoming is a vast area with few people in it. When I was small there were only about a quarter of a million in the whole state, with a tenth of them living in Cheyenne, the capital. Even today Wyoming has fewer than four hundred thousand people, and Cheyenne less than sixty-five thousand. In many towns it's hard to get enough boys of comparable age together for baseball or football, but all it takes to play basketball is a ball and a basket. Besides, the weather's bad and the summers are short. So, even though the kids love all sports, they play basketball more than anything else.

Basketball was always big in Wyoming. I started playing it when I was in the second or third grade and, although I was small and skinny—I just about make five feet, nine inches today—I loved the game and became pretty good at it. I had some natural ability and a knack for shooting with accuracy, and in my kid dreams I was always the hero in University of Wyoming victories.

But my dreams were not restricted to basketball. I was crazy about all sports, and devoured the sports pages and all the books about sports I could get my hands on. I was so nuts on the subject that it upset my mother, who was afraid I'd neglect my lessons, and I guess she had something there. I used to make up sports games and play them by the hour, often at the expense of homework. I had no brothers and my only sister is nine years younger than I, so I spent many an evening alone in my room, reading and dreaming about basketball and baseball and football and fishing and track and hockey and anything else that had a remote connection with sports.

My father was a good sports fan, and would have been a better one if he had the time. He came from Illinois and his favorite team was the Chicago Cubs, so they got to be my favorites, too. We couldn't get major league baseball on the air in those days—there were no game-of-the-week broadcasts or anything like that—but I followed the fortunes of the Cubs in the daily papers. At that time they had an outstanding team, well up in the National League races. They won pennants in 1929 and 1932, and among my heroes were Charlie Grimm and Billy Herman and Stan Hack and Billy Jurges and Guy Bush and Kiki Cuyler and Lon Warneke. Two of them, Jurges and Herman, later became close friends of mine as managers of the Red Sox. Sometimes, to my mother's annoyance, I spent hours talking baseball with my dad when he came home from work. He had sports dreams of his own—far less ambitious than mine but fully as hard to realize.

"Curtis," he used to say, "some day you and I are going back to Chicago and watch the Cubs in person."

Many years later I had the pleasure of taking him to big league games, but I don't think he ever got to see the Cubs.

He couldn't take me to Chicago but he could take me to Laramie for University of Wyoming basketball games. The Cowboys had a great team in 1934, when they nearly won the national championship, and we went to see them play once or twice a week. Those fellows were all heroes to me, and they intensified my dream to be a Wyoming star myself some day.

My favorite football team was Notre Dame, which won a national title under Knute Rockne in 1930. I could recite the names of all the regulars and the substitutes and the substitutes' substitutes on that team, and among its members was a very personal hero of mine. His name was Tom Kassis, and he was the guard opposite the immortal Bert Metzger, who won fame as the All-American watch charm guard. Kassis was neither as spectacular nor as well known, but he had one attraction which Metzger and everyone else at Notre Dame lacked. He lived in Cheyenne.

I pretty nearly drove Tom out of his mind with questions about Rockne and Metzger and Marty Brill and Frank Carideo and Marchy Schwartz and all the others on that great Irish team because I never stopped pumping him. I don't know how often I asked the same questions, but I couldn't help myself. I had to know everything there was to know, and I didn't ever want to forget any of it. Thank heaven for Tom's patience. He never seemed to run out of it. I guess he was just as glad to talk about Notre Dame as I was to hear about it.

In later years I did much the same thing to Bunny Oakes when he came to Wyoming to coach football after having coached Byron (Whizzer) White throughout White's college career, which started at Colorado in 1935 when I was sixteen years old. The world now knows White as one of the two Supreme Court justices appointed by the late President John F. Kennedy, but to me he was the great Whizzer, part man, part god.

I never met him—haven't met him to this day, in fact. The closest I ever got to him was in his senior year, 1937, when I drove down to Denver with another boy to see Colorado play Missouri. I sat in the stands with my eyes glued on this remarkable student-athlete, who not only made All-America that year but was also a Rhodes Scholar. Early in the game he made a quick kick of eighty-seven yards or some such fantastic distance, and during halftime I went down to where I could see the teams come out of their locker rooms.

White came by so close to me I could have touched him. It was one of those warm, beautiful September afternoons, with just enough breeze to ruffle a man's hair. White's was honey-colored, and as he came running out to the field with his helmet under his arm and his eyes straight ahead, he looked like a character out of Greek mythology.

I guess I drove Bunny Oakes out of his mind, too, for when he arrived at Laramie I used to take him fly fishing on one or another of those scores of wonderful streams around there, and pump him about Whizzer White. I still remember everything Bunny told me because, like a child wanting to hear the same story over and over, I kept making him say the same things again and again. I'm sure that before I was through I knew as much about White as Oakes did himself.

One reason I followed the fortunes of teams like Notre Dame and Colorado was that Wyoming had such horrible football. When I was a kid they did well to win two games a year. They opened the 1930 season by losing to Utah, 72–0, and between 1932 and 1933 they went through a stretch of nine straight games without scoring a point. They ended that streak with two touchdowns against Colorado, but lost by a 40–12 score. Then the Utah Aggies shut them out again.

While I dreamed of the Notre Dames and the Minnesotas and the Michigans and the Tulanes and the Southern Californias and all the other big national powerhouses, Wyoming was playing neighboring institutions, many of which lacked even local reputations. And when I didn't go over to Laramie to watch them get slaughtered by Colorado Teachers or Brigham Young or Montana State, I stayed home and listened to Southern California games on the radio.

Through a quirk in the airwaves we could get station KFI in Los Angeles, more than a thousand miles away on the other side of the Rocky Mountains. I heard most of the Southern Cal games, which, because of their national importance, were broadcast by the big-name announcers, men like Graham McNamee and Bill Stern and Ted Husing. Husing was my favorite because he obviously knew more football than any of the others, who were great color men but lacked his grasp of the game.

It was fashionable in those days for announcers to get all excited while describing the scenery and the weather and the celebrities on hand, but Husing didn't bother with that sort of thing. He would give you the blocks and the traps and the formations and the way the defenses were set, and do it in a marvelously smooth speaking voice. He must have had millions of fans all over the country, but none was as faithful as I, nor more admiring.

The first sports announcing I ever did was in my own room with the door closed. My dad gave me a football game where you shook the dice and guessed what was coming up. I pretended I was Ted Husing, announcing the plays with all their ramifications. I was the tailback for Wyoming, and I rigged up a schedule that included teams like Notre Dame and Pitt and Army and Minnesota and Southern Cal and other great college football elevens of the day.

Wyoming always won in the last seconds of the game when the tailback—me—intercepted a pass and ran eighty yards for a touchdown, or knifed through the line and into the open field for sixty-five, or went around end for ninety. And when it was over, Husing—me—described the crowds of deliriously happy Wyoming fans carrying the hero—me— off the field after the glorious victory over Michigan, or Tulane, or Minnesota.

The season ended with the Cowboys undefeated and going to the Rose Bowl where they always won, thanks to some brilliant maneuver by the tailback. The climax never changed—only the method of achieving it. Naturally, I was always the star tailback, as well as the great announcer who described the action. There was no question in my mind of the relative importance of the two. The tailback was the big man. I wanted first to be a hero on the field. It was only if by some unhappy chance I failed to make the team or suffered a crippling injury that I would settle for being the man behind the microphone. I just admired announcers like Ted Husing. I worshiped stars like Whizzer White.

My mother prevented my preoccupation with sports from becoming an obsession blotting out everything else, including my lessons. Her formal education stopped when she graduated from high school, but she was—and is—a voracious reader and a woman of great intelligence. One of the first things she did when we arrived in Cheyenne from Green River was get me a library card, and she made sure I used it. From the children's book stage up, she constantly checked on me, often going to the library with me to see that I had a supply of books for reading as well as studying.

"You must build up your vocabulary," she used to say, "and the only way to do it is to read. Remember, you're confined here to Wyoming and you don't have much chance to move around. The world is full of strange and interesting places, and since you can't visit them you must let books bring them to you. Perhaps you'll see them when you grow up, but by reading you can know about them now."

She was very strict about my reading, and kept me from cheating by reading my books herself and quizzing me on them. She didn't have to read the classics—she knew them already. In those days one of the most popular, and surely the most erudite radio program on the air was "Information Please," to which we always listened during dinner. I marveled at the number of times my mother came up with answers even before experts like John Kieran and F. P. Adams and Oscar Levant did, especially when the questions concerned quotations from the masters or snatches of poetry.

When I was about ten years old my mother made me take elocution lessons. My teacher was Mrs. Fern Herring, who later won considerable local fame as an oil painter. Mrs. Herring lived five or six blocks away, and there was nothing I hated more than my weekly visit to her house to recite the Gettysburg Address or Horatius at the Bridge or some other rhetorical classic.

"I don't mind reading," I told my mom, "and I don't mind studying my lessons. But why do I have to take elocution? I hate it and I don't see how I'll ever use it. Who's ever going to want to listen to me?"

"Let me tell you something, Curtis," she said. "Anything that you learn—any skill that you acquire—might come in handy some day. Mrs. Herring is teaching you how to get on your feet and express yourself in front of others. I don't care how much you hate it. You're going to keep doing it until Mrs. Herring is satisfied that you can do it properly."

Of course she was right—just how right we never realized then. I make my living talking to large groups of people. It's hard to judge how much Mrs. Herring might have prepared me for my present career, but those lessons I detested certainly did me no harm. They taught me not to be afraid to speak in public, and they gave me confidence and poise.

Now that I look back on it, I don't envy Mrs. Herring one bit. The toughest job that she had was to get kids like me to stand still. We'd all get up there and shift our feet around and make faces and twist our hands and twitch our shoulders. If she did nothing else, she showed me how to stand and where to put my hands and how to express myself without stammering and how to keep from wiggling around.

She also made me speak up so that I could be heard. Most kids mumble when they get on their feet, and I was no exception. Mrs. Herring didn't give me any of the voice exercises that modern teachers use, or show me how to form the vowels and how to enunciate each syllable and all that sort of thing, but she wouldn't stand for unintelligible speech. Before she was through with me I talked so that I could be heard clearly by everyone in the room. Maybe I didn't pronounce the vowels exactly right or get every syllable down pat, but at least my voice had volume. And even though I was far from being her star pupil and abhorred every minute I spent on her lessons I never forgot anything she taught me.

Nor did I ever forget how to touch-type, another skill my mother made me learn—and she did that practically over my dead body. I raised a terrible fuss about taking typing, not so much because I disliked it but because I knew I'd be the only boy in the class. Typing was for girls, and I wanted no part of it.

By then I was a senior in high school, a hotshot basket-ball player, a pretty good all-round athlete, a sports nut and a class officer, but girls frightened me to death. The only one I knew well was my sister Margaret and she was eight years old. I didn't want to know any others. I went to dances and mixed parties when I couldn't get out of it, but spent all the time there with boys. I went out on a date when forced to—sometimes I couldn't get out of that, either —but was too uncomfortable to enjoy myself and fled as soon as possible.

Around school I was always with boys. I sat beside them and walked from class to class with them and had lunch with them and met them after school on the ball field or in the gymnasium. I didn't understand girls and wanted nothing to do with them. The only time I ever saw much of them outside the classroom was one year when I went in for dramatics—that was my mother's idea, too. In one scene I had to put my arms around a girl, and almost died.

So you can imagine how I felt when, just before I went back to school for my senior year my mother said one day, "Curtis, I want you to take typewriting."

"Typewriting?" I yelled. "I'm not going to take typewriting. That's for girls."

"You *are* going to take typewriting," she said. "Everyone should know how to type."

"Every girl, maybe," I said. "But what good is it to a boy?"

"You can't tell," she said. "Some day you might put it to very good use."

"What do you think I'm going to be—a secretary or something?" I said. "That's the only good anyone could get out of it. And who wants a male secretary?"

"There are lots of other things a competent typist can do besides being a secretary," she said. "And it's no disgrace for a man to be a competent typist."

"Not this man," I said. "I'd be the only one in a whole roomful of girls. I'll be a sissy if I take typing—the boys will call me a sissy and the girls will make fun of me. I won't do it."

"Yes, you will," she said firmly.

So I took typing, the only boy in the whole of Cheyenne High School who did. There were about thirty-five girls and me in a class which, of course, was taught by a woman. The first day, I tried to sneak in after everyone else was settled and had to look all around for a seat. The teacher finally pointed one out in the middle of the room, and I slunk into it like a condemned man in the electric chair. The girls giggled and even the teacher had to suppress a smile.

After that I rushed to be the first one in the room so I could take a seat way in the back. Even there I wasn't comfortable. The girls called me the "male secretary," and somebody was always kidding me. I happened to blush very easily, so my face was nearly always beet red by the time the class began. But the teacher was understanding, and after a while everyone got used to my being there. Before I was through I could type about sixty words a minute. Just as my mother had predicted, this turned out to be a godsend. I have to do a tremendous amount of writing in my work and I don't always have the use of a secretary. Being able to touch-type has saved me innumerable hours of precious time.

Although I was a pretty good student I fooled around in class the way most kids did in the days before getting into college was practically a matter of life and death. I liked to sit near a window or a door so if I got bored when the weather was nice I could duck out without the teacher seeing me. I never really played hooky because I always showed up for the next class, but I liked to wander around or relax in the sun for a few minutes on those wonderful Wyoming mornings in the autumn or the spring.

I got really restless in the early weeks of my senior year, and my marks started to fall off. My mother didn't expect straight A's from me, but she insisted I do well in English. Instead, as the opening of the basketball season approached, I got worse and worse, largely because I didn't do any work.

One day my English teacher said, "I don't know what's come over you, Curtis, but you're doing very poorly. You're obviously not even studying, and I'm going to write a note to your mother."

I had to deliver the note myself, and when she read it my mother glared and demanded an explanation.

"I'll be all right," I said.

"You'll be all right, all right," she said. "I'm going over to see the principal tomorrow and tell him you can't play basketball until you *are* all right."

"Can't play basketball?" I exclaimed. "Mom, we've got a great team. Maybe we'll win the state championship. Practice starts in a couple of days. You can't do this to me."

"I not only can, but I will," she said.

The next day she saw the principal, and he called me in and said, "You're restricted from basketball. Your grades are terrible and if you want to play you'd better do something about them."

"Gee," I said, "I *have* to play basketball."

"You have to get your mother's permission first," he said. "And she won't give it until you improve in your work."

I walked out of his office with tears in my eyes. I was mad at him and mad at my English teacher and maddest of all at my mother, and for a couple of days I wouldn't talk to anyone. Basketball was the only thing in the world that meant anything to me, and they were taking it away from me. But I finally realized the only way I could play was to get my marks up, so I really dug into the books. The English teacher gave us weekly tests, and I got a 95 on the first one, which came a few days after basketball practice began. The next week I got a 98, and she gave me another note to take to my mother. When Mom read it she smiled and said, "All right, Curtis, you can go out for basketball tomorrow."

She was always after me about my clothes because she wanted me to look nice in school, especially on Fridays, when we had assembly for the whole student body—pretty nearly one thousand pupils. My favorite outfit was an old shirt and a pair of dirty white corduroy pants full of other kids' signatures. I wore them for a couple of years and they must have had three-hundred names on them. When my mother threatened to throw them out, I hid them in the tool shed behind the garage, and when I left for school looking too neat for my own taste I stopped by and changed into them.

One Friday morning my mother made me put on a clean white shirt and a necktie and my best suit, and saw that my shoes were shined and my fingernails clean. I said, "Mom, what's the idea? It's only a school day."

"It's assembly day," she said. "And I want you to look like a gentleman."

I went out the back door, then, making sure she wasn't looking, I ducked into the tool shed and changed into the corduroys and the old shirt, leaving my suit and shirt and necktie hanging on hooks. Then I went off to school.

The assembly that morning was to induct newly elected students into the National Honor Society, and a lot of parents were there. When I went in with my class I noticed that not only my mother, but my father, too, was among those present. I thought that was funny, because he had to leave work, and I didn't see any particular reason for him to make such an effort to be there.

Walt Oslund, the president of the school, stood up on the platform and made the announcement about the National Honor Society, and somebody else gave a little talk, and then they began calling out names. I sat back, figuring this was one thing that had nothing to do with me. My grades had been pretty good, and I had taken part in several extracurricular activities and was an athlete, but I was forever in hot water with one teacher or another for fooling around in class.

But my mother knew something I didn't know. The night before the assembly, the principal had phoned to tell her I had made the Society. That was why my father had taken time off to go to the assembly and she had insisted I get so dressed up.

When my name was called I was too stunned to move. All I could think was, "Oh boy, I have to go up there in front of all these people in this old shirt and these dirty cords, with Mom and Dad sitting out there watching me." They had to call my name a second time before I stood up and sheepishly shuffled to the platform. The only things on me that looked right were my shoes and my fingernails.

At first I didn't dare look at my parents. Then I stole a peek at them and saw they were beaming with pride. And when I got home that night, all Mom said was, "Curtis, I do wish you'd stay dressed up on assembly days."

2

My closest pals growing up were Willie Rothman and Leon (Stretch) Brown. The three of us were inseparable. We were the same age and in the same school grade, and we shared the same interests, especially basketball. We also shared the same dreams—dreams of dazzling success on the field of sport. Our most immediate hope when we entered high school was to make the basketball team, but when we looked into the more distant future we could see ourselves starring for the University of Wyoming, and helping our beloved Cowboys win the national championship.

Our ambitions to make the high school team were more than dreams. We were all good basketball players in an age when height wasn't particularly important. I was the smallest of the three, for when I entered high school I stood only about five feet, five and weighed 115 pounds. But I had worked all my life at dribbling and running and shooting, and got to be pretty good at all three.

At that time everyone was taught to shoot with both hands, but I found it easier to get up close to the basket and shoot with one. As a matter of fact, I guess I was the only kid in town who could shoot that way. When John Powell, the high school coach, first saw me do it he tried to discourage me, but after he realized I could shoot accurately with one hand he didn't try to stop me.

I started in my junior year as a reserve on the varsity, and when I scored six baskets in one quarter against Douglas High I was designated as the sixth man. This meant I would be first off the bench when anyone came out of the game, but I was too small to fill in at center. Powell was always after me to get some flesh on my bones. I ate huge meals and slurped up fantastic quantities of ice cream sodas and sundaes, and I took stretching and body-building exercises, but nothing did much good. I was fated to be little, and I continued to be the runt of the basketball team.

At one point the coach suggested I run on the track team because I was pretty fast and he thought it would strengthen my wind. He even came over to the house one time to talk to my mother about it.

"Well," Mom said, "I guess it would be up to Curtis, but I'm against it. I think basketball keeps him busy enough."

That didn't exactly leave it up to Curtis, but I wasn't crazy about the idea anyhow. Track and basketball overlapped. Besides, I had plenty of other sports interests—hunting, fishing, baseball, football, and tennis. I played whatever was in season, and basketball was always in season to me.

We had a real good basketball team in my senior year of high school. Bill Cook and I were the forwards and the smallest men on the club; he was just a bit taller than I. A boy named Bob Kenworthy, who stood around six feet, six inches, was the center, and my old buddies, Willie Rothman and Stretch Brown, both around six feet, two, were the guards. Fred Ziegler, another boy with whom I grew up, was the sixth man.

We lost our first two games, but then won thirty-seven straight, and went to Casper for the state tournament as favorites to win the championship, with Rock Springs High close behind. Rock Springs, a coal-mining town of about ten thousand in the southwestern part of Wyoming, were the defending champions. Their star was Bill Strannigan, who later roomed with me at Wyoming and is now the Wyoming basketball coach.

Everyone who followed high school basketball in the state figured neither Rock Springs nor we would have any trouble reaching the semi-finals. Our first-round opponents were

Rawlins High, a team we had murdered twice already. But in the locker room before the game we were as tight as fiddle strings. Usually, we laughed and kidded around while we dressed, but this time nobody said much of anything. And when we tossed the ball around while working out on the floor, we were missing passes and shooting cold.

That was the last year of the center jump—1937—and when the game began the tip came to me. I passed the ball to Willie who turned to throw it to Stretch, down near the Rawlins basket. The ball went right through Stretch's hands and hit him in the face, and a Rawlins player got it and they went down to score. Then we got the ball again and started down the court with it. My opponent was guarding me a little too closely, and I faked him out of position and went in wide open for an easy layup. There wasn't a Rawlins boy within twenty feet of me, and there I was, the leading schoolboy scorer in the state, all by myself under the basket with the ball in my hand.

It wasn't possible for anybody to miss a shot like that, but I managed to. The ball hit the rim and rolled around, then bounced out. A Rawlins boy grabbed it and off they went to another score. They were seven or eight points ahead of us before we started getting back on the track, but we never were really right. It was just one of those nights when everything went wrong.

We rallied a bit near the end of the game, but by then it was too late. Even though we came up with a couple of quick baskets we lost, 37–34, and that was the end of our hopes for a state championship. We dragged ourselves off the floor and went into the locker room and cried—all of us from the coach down. Poor John was so unhappy that there were tears in his eyes for the rest of the tournament. To his dying day, he never forgot that first-round beating we took from a team we usually put into our back pockets. Years later, just before he passed away, he told me it was the biggest disappointment of his coaching career.

After we graduated from high school in 1937, Willie, Stretch, and I decided to work for a year before entering college. Aside from the fact that we could use the money, we felt—and our parents agreed with us, although it wasn't their idea—that another year of growth, physical and otherwise, would more than make up for what we might lose by not going to college right away. The other two were tall enough, but very skinny, and I was practically scrawny. Furthermore, I just didn't have the emotional maturity for college. More kid than man, I had no experience with the world outside my own little orbit and no real sense of responsibility.

I got a job at the Union Pacific Railroad as an electrician's apprentice for 37½ cents an hour, eight hours a day, five days a week. I loved the work, which was mostly servicing streamliners traveling between Chicago and the West Coast. Everything stopped in Cheyenne for thorough checking, since we were right in the middle.

There was romance in all of those beautiful, sleek, air-conditioned trains, and whenever I worked on one I thought of where it was going and where it had been. Except for an occasional trip into Colorado or Utah I had never been out of Wyoming in my life, and here I was working on trains that traveled between Chicago and either San Francisco or Los Angeles. I envied crew and passengers alike.

I never really got to talking to many of them, for my job kept me under the trains, not in them. There were belts that drove the generators, and a gang of us would have perhaps twenty minutes to half an hour to inspect them. We had to work fast, especially if anything needed adjusting, because the railroad's great pride was its ability to maintain a tight schedule almost to the minute.

Occasionally I got through in time to wander over to the diner, where the chef, if he liked you, would slip you a roast beef sandwich or something. I had many a lunch or between-meal snack off a Union Pacific diner.

I also had plenty of time for recreation. I went fishing every chance I got, and played a lot of tennis and softball. During the winter that we took off from school Willie and Stretch and I played on the Elks Club basketball team. We won the state amateur championship and went to Denver for the nationals, where we were beaten in the first round. But it was good experience and nowhere nearly as morale-shattering as that high school loss to Rawlins had been.

In those days softball was a big sport in most sections of the country, and Cheyenne had so many players that the league was divided into classes. During my second summer out of school I pitched and played in the outfield for a team sponsored by Thompson's billiard hall in the Class A league. There were just a few of us in my age bracket. Most of the fellows were working men in their mid-twenties, and a couple were over thirty. Some worked for the railroad, and one, George Halverson, was a mailman. Halverson was a wonderful center fielder, as good an outfielder as I've ever seen even after years of watching big league baseball. If he could hit—which he couldn't—I'm sure he would have been a major leaguer.

We played two or three games a week and won the state softball title. This earned us the right to represent Wyoming in the national softball championships at Chicago, only first we had to get there. We didn't have much money, and, although those of us who worked for the railroad might have wangled free transportation, we couldn't have raised nearly enough to pay the rest of the fares.

But a couple of the boys had cars, and Mr. Thompson gave us money for gas and oil and maybe a few extras. We still had to scrounge around town for the rest of our expenses. We might be in Chicago anywhere from two to five days, depending on how long we lasted in the tournament. We scraped up enough cash to keep us there about three, and took off.

It was a marvelously crazy trip—a thrill, yet an ordeal.

The mid-August weather was boiling hot. As soon as we reached the prairies the thermometer climbed up over 100 and stayed there all the way to Chicago. We couldn't afford to stop anywhere overnight, so we drove straight through. We traveled six in a car, taking turns driving, and living on hamburgers, hot dogs, soda pop, and snacks. We didn't sleep much, partly because we couldn't, but mostly because nobody wanted to miss anything.

If I'm not mistaken, there wasn't a man on the team who had ever been east of the Mississippi and few who had been even that far, so the trip alone was a wonderful adventure for us all. On top of that was the prospect of seeing the nation's second biggest city, and of meeting people from all over the country. We all looked forward to the tournament itself, and had high hopes of really doing well. And I was especially thrilled because I had been hearing about Chicago all my life. Besides, the Cubs would be in town when we were, and I couldn't wait to watch them play. Neither could any of the others, none of whom had ever seen a big league ball game.

We pulled into town at noon on the day before the tournament, after more than forty hours on the road. The tournament committee had arranged for us to stay at a small hotel near the Loop where the price was right and we could sleep four in a room. I was surprised they let us in. We must have been the most beat-up looking ball club of all time. We needed shaves, showers, and clean clothes and couldn't remember when we had last slept in beds.

But we were too excited to be tired. We had just time enough to leave our luggage and rush out to Wrigley Field for the Cubs game. Afterwards, we hung around the players' gate for autographs, and when we got back to town it was time for dinner. We found a cheap place to eat and then, like the true yokels we were, spent the evening at a burlesque show. We finally fell into bed at midnight and slept like dead men until we had to get up the next day for the start of the tournament.

We dressed at the hotel and drove out to one of the high school fields, where we were to play the Pennsylvania champions, from Pittsburgh, in the first round. We didn't look much better in our uniforms than in street clothes. They were the same ones we had worn all season, and, despite a free cleaning and pressing by one of the local laundries, they could hardly be described as sharp.

Across the front were the words, "Thompson's Billiard Hall," but the letters were faded and torn, and so were those on the back that identified us as from Cheyenne. The laundry had done its best, but no pressing job could have withstood that trip in the heat of Nebraska, Iowa, and western Illinois. I guess we looked pretty bad, but the crowd greeted us with a combination of good-natured cheers and cowboy yips.

The Pittsburgh boys, on the other hand, really looked the part of champions. They had brand-new uniforms and were zinging a ball around the infield when we arrived. If clothes and fancy infield practice made the ball club, we wouldn't have had a chance. Fortunately, they don't.

We had a pretty good team and a great pitcher, a rubber-armed southpaw named Murray Stovall who was absolutely tireless. The only times I ever pitched were when Murray couldn't get to the ball park. Unlike most good softball pitchers, who have marvelous fast balls, he didn't have great speed, but his breaking stuff was almost unhittable. And the longer he pitched the better he got. I had often seen him work both ends of a doubleheader and strike out more men in the second game than he had in the first.

Which was why I played left field most of the time, and that's where I played in the Chicago tournament.

A surprisingly large crowd—about six thousand people—turned out for the game because the Pittsburgh boys were among the favorites to win the tournament, and their pitcher was famous for his blazing fast ball. He and Stovall started out in a battle of strikeouts. They dominated the first four innings of the seven-inning game. In the fifth we finally broke through with a run, and we picked up another in the sixth. Pittsburgh finally nicked Stovall for a run in their half of the sixth, but Murray shut them out in the seventh, and we won a stunning upset victory by a 2–1 score.

Our first reaction was relief that we hadn't been knocked out of the tournament in the first round. On the way back to the hotel somebody said, "Well, boys, we can stay around another day." That night there was a big affair for all the softball players—the girls' championships were also being held—and the poor but proud cowboys from Wyoming had a wonderful time. Everybody lionized us and called us the Cinderella team of the tournament because we had beaten this great Pittsburgh team.

The next day there was an even bigger crowd out to watch us play the top favorites, the Florida champions from Clearwater. They hadn't been beaten all year, and one look at their pitcher was all we needed to figure out why. He could throw a softball faster than any man I ever saw. The ball blazed across the plate like a bullet.

Stovall wasn't quite so effective as he had been the day before, but he got fantastic support. Halverson made some miraculous catches in center field, and nothing within reasonable reach got through the infield. Neither team scored for six innings, but then we came through with a couple in the seventh. To everybody's amazement, we won another 2–1 upset victory.

So on the way back to the hotel we were still repeating, "Another day in Chicago. We're not out yet."

None of us mentioned it, but we all knew the next day would be the last we could afford. If we won again we'd have to wire home for money.

The Chicago newspapers, which had been giving the tournament good coverage, really went overboard on us the next morning. The softball stories all featured the unknown cowboys from Cheyenne who had knocked off two top favorites on successive days and were threatening to steal all the marbles.

It made us feel great. It would have made us feel greater if we had known where our next meal was coming from.

When we reached the ball park the next day for the third-round game, against the Virginia champions from Richmond, we were greeted by the biggest crowd we'd seen. There were over ten thousand people on hand, and, judging by the yips and applause, most of them were cheering for us.

Richmond wasn't supposed to be as good as either Pittsburgh or Clearwater, so we were favorites to win. The tireless Stovall pitched for the third straight day, and he set down the Virginia boys like tenpins for five innings. Both teams scored in the sixth and when Richmond came up for the last of the seventh the game was tied.

They got a man on third with one out when the batter hit a Texas Leaguer to left, a pop-up too deep for the shortstop and apparently too shallow for me in left field. But I broke and came in fast, then reached forward and grabbed the ball at my shoetops, maybe the best catch I ever made in my life. I followed with the worst boner. I was so thrilled at the brilliance of the catch that I momentarily forgot about the man on third. He tagged up and, when he saw that I was off balance, headed for the plate. I ate the ball while just about everybody in the park was yelling for me to throw home. By the time I got around to doing that the baserunner had scored.

So I blew the game because that was the last run either team scored that day. When it was over a big, beefy, red-faced guy rushed up to me and yelled, "I've been watching you guys play and telling everybody about you and cheer-

ing for you and betting on you, and you lost the ball game.
You ought to be ashamed of yourself."

I just looked at him a second and said, "Thanks," then
walked away. He was the only one who squawked. Not a
man on the team had a word of criticism for me and no
mention of my bloop was ever again mentioned in anger.
In the years that followed we kidded about it, but that was
all.

As a matter of fact, it was just as well we lost. We had to
pool our resources to pay the hotel bill the next morning,
and then we drove back to Cheyenne on short rations. And
when we arrived we were greeted as heroes because everyone in town had followed the tournament and the people
were all proud and happy we had done so well.

I entered the University of Wyoming in the fall of 1938.
I had always loved Laramie and had been looking forward
to going there to college all my life. The city, seven thousand feet above sea level, is a sportman's paradise and the
university a student's dream. We had about two thousand
undergraduates and I guess every one of us, girls and boys
alike, was crazy about the place.

The campus, with its granite buildings and its spotless
grass and its marvelous views of the surrounding mountains, was and is magnificent. You can hunt and fish and
picnic and ski and skate and enjoy all sorts of other outdoor activities within a few miles of the school. We used to
have our dances—well-chaperoned—up in the Snowy Range
or the Glacier Peaks, not far from the university.

One of the things I liked best about Laramie was that
you never needed much spare time to go fishing because
there were little streams all over the place. We'd take off for
an hour or so, which we couldn't do in Cheyenne because it
took that long to come and go. Everybody dressed the same
for fishing—in boots and levis—so you never knew if you
were with a millionaire rancher or one of his hired hands.
You didn't care, either.

In the fall I went duck hunting with my accounting professor, a wonderful guy named Claire Mundell. We'd get up early and have our limit of ducks in time to get back for 8 A.M. classes. I did that morning after morning in the duck season all the way through my four years of college. I wouldn't miss a day of hunting with Claire if my life depended on it.

In the spring I'd get through classes at three in the afternoon, and go fishing and be back by six with a full basket of trout. Sometimes Walter Brown, my mother's cousin, who was the engineer of a Union Pacific streamliner and a marvelous fly fisherman, would come over to spend a couple of hours with me. Walter knew more about trout than any man I ever met. He taught me just about everything I know about them today.

My preoccupation with outdoor sports didn't interfere with my passion for athletics in general, or with my ambitions to play basketball. We didn't have a formal freshman team, but played other teams around Laramie and worked out with the varsity. The dream of my life was to play in "Hell's Half Acre," the university gym. The place was named after a desolate and huge area in Wyoming where rustlers used to hide, not because it was desolate but because it was huge. Our Hell's Half Acre was one of the biggest basketball courts in the United States.

It was worth about ten points to us in every game because we were used to its dimensions and visiting teams weren't. And clubs that came from lower altitudes were really in trouble. The thin air at seven thousand feet, which we took for granted, left them breathless after a while. That and all the running they had to do on the big court made every game an uphill battle for them.

When I first went out for the varsity in my sophomore year Wyoming had a new coach named Ev Shelton, who had already won considerable fame as a schoolboy and amateur team coach. Just before coming to Laramie he had won national A.A.U. championships with a Denver team, so everyone in the area knew who he was.

I made the varsity as a sophomore, but that didn't mean much because we had a weak team. As a matter of fact, the freshmen, with two outstanding boys, Kenny Sailors and Jim Weir, were better than we were. Both helped us through fine seasons in the next two years. Sailors was an All-American forward who later starred in professional basketball.

We won the Rocky Mountain Conference championships with ten wins and two losses in my junior year, and then went to Kansas City for the western regional finals. Sailors and I were forwards, Weir the center, my boyhood pal Willie Rothman and Strannigan the guards, and Chuck Benson the sixth man. We had about everything but height, and that kept us from going very far in national tournament play. Weir was the only man over six feet two inches. Sailors was five-ten, and at five-eight and a half, I was the smallest.

The trip to Kansas City was at the other end of the social scale from that softball trip to Chicago. We went first class all the way, stopped at the best hotel in town, lived on steaks instead of hot dogs, and never had to worry about how long we'd have to stay. If each one of us had been about five inches taller, we might have gone the distance.

But our first-round opponents were the Arkansas Razorbacks, whose shortest man, Red Hickey, stood six-four. Hickey later was coach of the professional San Francisco 49ers football team. The Arkansas center, Pops Friedberger, stood six-ten. We didn't have much chance to win, but we gave them a pretty good ball game, losing only by nine or ten points. The next night Creighton beat us by a point in the consolation round.

We thought we'd have a real shot at the national championship my senior year because we figured to be even stronger than the year before. All the regulars were still around, plus a six-seven sophomore named Milo Komenich, from Gary, Indiana. He was the only out-of-state boy on the squad. Wyoming never went far afield for athletes, but we welcomed Milo with open arms. He represented height, and we needed that more than anything else.

But we got off to a slow start, and didn't really begin to roll until the season was about a third old. By then we had lost close games on the road to Brigham Young, Utah, and Colorado, which had a great team that year. We finally got organized and won our last nine straight, finishing up with a victory over Colorado, but we were too late. Colorado won the conference championship and we ended up second.

That was the end of my basketball career, but we all had other worries at that point.

My roommate, Bill Strannigan, had just gotten married, and worked in a filling station in Laramie. There wasn't much to do on Sundays, so I used to drop in on him from time to time. One day we were sitting around with the radio going in the background when the music stopped and an announcer cut in with the story that changed the lives and hopes and ambitions of us all.

It was December 7, 1941, and the Japanese had just attacked Pearl Harbor.

3

I had been in the university R.O.T.C., and after Pearl Harbor I applied for the Army Air Force. In January of 1942 I went to Denver for my physical. When I passed it I was told to go back to college and wait for orders, which wouldn't come through at least until after I graduated in June. As an R.O.T.C. man I'd get a commission in the Army Reserve with my degree anyhow. If I didn't go directly into the Air Force, I could transfer into it later.

In the meantime, I bought a jalopy for ten dollars from a guy at school. Even at that price it was hardly a bargain. The car was an ancient Model A Ford with no top, thin brakes, and a cracked block. I figured I could manage the brakes, but I had to get the block fixed or the car wouldn't run. Andy Bugas, whose brother John later became a vice president of the Ford Motor Company, helped me weld it, and I was in business.

Now, for the first time in my life, I could go fishing whenever I felt like it instead of depending on somebody else to take me. I've had dozens of cars since, but none I was ever prouder of. I drove around town in that beat-up old mess as though it were a brand-new Rolls-Royce.

The brakes were so terrible that I had to strain and push like mad to get them to work. Even then it was necessary to slow down well in advance of an anticipated stop. The only place I could step on the gas with any feeling of safety was on the open road, but I had to get ready for my turnoff half a mile beforehand or I'd miss it.

After a while I began waking up mornings with a stiff back, but I didn't pay any attention to it. I played baseball that spring, and noticed a twinge in my back whenever I went down for a ground ball, but I still didn't let it bother me. I kept on driving the old Ford and fighting the brakes, never connecting those daily battles with whatever might be wrong with my back.

I stayed in Laramie waiting for orders after I graduated because it was closer to the trout streams and I wouldn't have to drive so far to go fishing. I got a job waiting on tables in the cocktail lounge of the Hotel Conner, the only night work I could find so I could fish all day and still earn a little money before I went into the service. A couple of other boys who had just graduated with me were also around town waiting for orders, and they went with me whenever they had time.

It was a lazy existence which would have been ideal except for the war. But we knew we'd be called up pretty soon, so we practically lived by those little mountain streams while we could. We'd have plenty of time to miss them after we got into uniform.

I kept right on driving the old heap with its bad brakes, and kept right on fighting them whenever I wanted to slow or stop. My back didn't get worse, but it didn't get better either. By the time my orders arrived in midsummer, I was used to waking up in pain. However, just before reporting for duty I had the family doctor in Cheyenne take a look at me.

He decided I had a touch of arthritis and gave me a couple of vitamin injections. Then, along with the other boys who had hung around Laramie with me and who had the same infantry orders that I did, I headed for Camp Edwards, on Cape Cod. It was my first trip to the East Coast, and the longest I had ever taken in my life.

We changed trains in Chicago, reached Boston two nights and three days after leaving home, then took a bus to the Cape. By the time we arrived there my back seemed in pretty good shape. The shots and all those hours away from the jalopy apparently paid off.

I got along fine for a while, although the training, which was for amphibious duty, was tough and demanding. I even had a chance to go up to Boston to watch big league baseball a few times. I saw Ted Williams hit a home run in Fenway Park one day, and another time saw poor old Jimmy Foxx try to stretch himself beyond his physical limits. By then, old and through after a great American League career, he was with the Cubs.

That was the last ball game I saw in Boston for a long time. A few days later, in the midst of one of those big back bends that were part of our daily routine of calisthenics, there was a funny little noise and I could feel something give, and then a searing pain shot down my leg. I couldn't move at all for a couple of minutes, then finally managed to get up, but that was the end of the exercises as far as I was concerned.

I hoped maybe the pain would go away overnight, but it was worse the next morning, so I reported at sick call. The doctor, a young guy fresh out of medical school who threw around some of the long words he had learned there as though he had invented them, asked me a lot of questions. When he got through examining my back and leg he told me there wasn't anything wrong that stretching wouldn't cure.

"We'll put you to sleep in the hospital and get those muscles loosened up," he said. "You'll be all right in a couple of days."

While I was in the hospital my orders came through to report to Maxwell Field in Montgomery, Alabama for flight training. My back didn't feel any better after the stretching treatment than it had before. But I was so anxious to go to Montgomery that I told the Edwards people I was all right, so they let me check out of there.

The train trip south was agony. My back got worse by the hour, and when I finally arrived I could hardly walk.

Those Air Force guys must have been delighted to see me. Here I was, limping along, obviously in pain, hardly able to straighten up, reporting for duty that required what was then the toughest training in the service. But I told them it wasn't anything serious and I'd be all right in the morning.

The next day I couldn't do even the simplest calisthenics. The drill officer was a real tough guy, and I guess he thought I was faking at first, but after he watched me try to go through the motions awhile even he realized there was something radically wrong. He sent me to the doctor, who put me through the same routine of questions and examinations the young guy at Edwards had. Finally he said, "I'm not sure what's wrong with you, but we'll put you in the hospital and see if a few days' rest won't fix you up."

To this day, I think my back might have been all right if the Edwards doctor had done that instead of stretching my muscles. In later years, back specialists told me I had lesions which probably never would have been there if the first Army doctor who examined me had handled me properly.

But by the time I reached Montgomery I guess there wasn't much anyone could do. I was in the hospital there for several weeks, but nobody seemed to know what was wrong, or at least they never told me. One day I heard the nurses say something about a ruptured disc. I had never heard the phrase and didn't have the foggiest notion what it was. I asked the doctor, and he said he still didn't know if that was my trouble.

They finally let me leave the hospital, but I couldn't return to active duty because my back hurt as much as ever. Montgomery was jammed at that time, so the Air Force people arranged for me to stay in a private home. I was limping around, checking in at the hospital every weekday and still in terrific pain.

One day the landlady told me a good friend of hers with trouble similar to mine had been successfully treated by a

world-famous Baltimore neurosurgeon named Dr. Walter
Dandy. I wrote him, asking for a Saturday appointment,
and when he gave me one I got a weekend pass and went to
Baltimore on my own. Both Dr. Dandy and Dr. George
Bennett, a well-known orthopedic surgeon, agreed that I
had a ruptured disc.

"The only thing that will cure you is an operation," Dr.
Dandy said. "You'll never get rid of that pain without one."

When I told the Army doctors what he had said they
gave me hell for going to Baltimore at all. According to
them, I had no right to see any civilian doctor without
their permission.

"I'm sorry," I said. "Only what are you going to do
about my back? It's been this way for weeks. I've still got
bad pain, and nobody has decided anything. I'm not doing
the Air Force any good in this condition. Anything anybody
can do to change it will have my everlasting gratitude, but
please, somebody do something."

A few more weeks went by, and still nothing happened.
Then they brought me up before a medical board and began talking about assigning me to limited duty.

"Look," I said. "I don't want limited duty. I want to get
back to regular duty and be active. I want to learn to fly
and go overseas. I'd rather take my chances with a sound
back than go through the war on limited duty. Can't you
operate or something?"

Whether they could or not, they seemed impressed, and
the chairman said they would see what could be worked
out. In the meantime, since I couldn't do anything around
the field, they gave me a Christmas leave to go home and
told me they'd decide what to do with me after I got back.

It was a long haul to Cheyenne, and once again every turn
of the train wheels nearly killed me. I was in such pain
when I got home that as soon as Christmas was over, I
went to an Army hospital in nearby Fort Warren to see
what they could do. They transferred me to Fitzsimons

General Hospital in Denver, and I stayed there a couple of months, while the doctors continued to try to dope out what to do with me.

I told the neurosurgeon who examined me from time to time what Dr. Dandy had said, and he agreed that the diagnosis might be correct. But after a long series of tests, he said, "If you've got a ruptured disc I'll eat it. That's one thing I'm sure you haven't got."

It took him another month or so to decide what he thought I did have. He finally came to the conclusion that it was spinal arthritis, and in the spring of 1943 he gave me a medical discharge.

So my entire Army career lasted about eight months, half of which I spent in hospitals. When I got back to Cheyenne I was the saddest sack in town. All my ambitions to become a flier were out the window, I was a wartime cripple without a Purple Heart, an Army veteran without a month of basic training. The nearest I had been to Europe was Camp Edwards. I hadn't even been up in an Army plane, much less learned to fly one. What a war hero I was!

On top of everything else, my back was still killing me. I went to see the family doctor, who told me to rest a few weeks. That didn't do any good either. "Curt," he said one day, "you're still limping around and in such pain you can't work or even loaf comfortably, and I honestly don't know what's wrong. I trained at the Mayo Clinic, and I think that's the place for you to go. If you really have a ruptured disc, as Dr. Dandy thought, they can operate there, and if you haven't maybe they can find out what you do have. But there isn't anything I can do for you, and I doubt if any other doctor in this part of the country can help you."

So he got me an appointment at the Mayo Clinic and I borrowed enough money from my dad to get to Rochester, Minnesota and back. When I arrived I was practically doubled up from train rides that included an agonizing wait in Chicago to make connections. The Mayo people didn't waste any time, but put me through a whole series of examinations and tests, some of which were pretty painful. But I was so sick I didn't care what they did as long as there was a chance they could relieve me.

A couple of days after I got there they confirmed Dr. Dandy's diagnosis and advised surgery. I couldn't wait for them to put me to sleep and do the job. It was performed by Dr. James Love, who later became Mayo's chief neurosurgeon and one of the world's foremost authorities. I found out afterward that some of my spinal nerve roots had been irreparably damaged by that stretching at Camp Edwards, and I guess that was why I didn't get any immediate benefits from the disc operation.

For I was just as unhappy after it as I had been before. The pain seemed even worse than it had been, and I had continual burning sensations in both legs. I couldn't eat or sleep or anything else, and now I didn't know which way to turn.

"Go back to Cheyenne," the Mayo doctors told me. "Don't do a thing for three months. By then you should be more comfortable."

So I didn't do a thing for three months and drove everyone around me crazy, including my mother, my dad, and Margaret, my little sister. I didn't see anybody or go anywhere and the few guys still around town got sick of coming to see me. All they heard was the same old story, because the only thing I could think or talk about was my aching back.

My father financed me to another trip to Mayo after three months, and they put me through some more examinations and tests. By then it was early September and the only thing I had done for six months was groan and growl and gripe and feel sorry for myself. But the Mayo doctors did give me a ray of hope. They said there were definite indications of improvement in my back and that if I would be patient and rest a few weeks longer they were sure my trouble would clear up.

Now it was the autumn of 1943, and the football season, such as it was, had begun. I sat at the radio and listened to any game I could get, high school, service, college— whatever was on the air. And, somewhat to my surprise after all I had been through, the pains started to subside. After a while, I walked around town, dropped in on friends, and showed signs of feeling human again.

I got into the habit of stopping in at the sports department of the Wyoming *Eagle*, and they offered me a part-time job covering schoolboy games. I wasn't the world's greatest sportswriter, but I wasn't the worst either. I loved being around athletes and, since I couldn't be one myself any more, writing about them seemed the next best thing.

But I preferred talking about them. Sometimes I went to my room, closed the door, and practiced broadcasting games I had covered, using my notes for details. One day Mom heard me, and came into the room.

"Curtis," she said, "you have a good voice and you're an expert on sports. Why don't you go down to station KFBC and see if they can use you? They must be as short of announcers as the *Eagle* is of reporters. Bill Grove, the manager, knows you. He used to broadcast Wyoming basketball games. Go down and have a talk with him. Work for nothing if you have to."

Bill Grove didn't have any paying jobs, but he said I could work with Frank Thomas, who did the Cheyenne High School play-by-play. This suited me fine because I covered most of those games for the *Eagle*, and it tied right in with my newspaper job. Frank had no objections —in fact, he was glad to have somebody to fill in the dead spots—so everybody was happy.

Cheyenne High was the only public secondary school in town, but there was a little parochial school called St. Mary's High which used an old field a few blocks from where I lived. They didn't have enough players for a full eleven, but they had a six-man team, and played a few games with other six-man teams nearby.

Somebody at KFBC got the bright idea of selling radio time for the last six-man game of the season, between St. Mary's and a team from the neighboring town of Pine Bluffs. By billing the game as for the six-man team championship of eastern Wyoming, the station sold time to about twenty Cheyenne merchants at five bucks apiece.

A couple of days before the game, Bill Grove said, "Curt, how would you like to do some play-by-play?"

"I'd love it," I said.

"O.K.," he said. "We need somebody to broadcast the six-man football game Saturday. Frank will be busy with the high school game."

"Six-man football?" I said.

"Do it just as if it were regular football," he said. "Do you want to try?"

I said I'd do it, but I wasn't very enthusiastic. My friends had read my stories in the *Eagle* and heard me do color on the regular high school broadcasts. I was a pretty important guy, I thought. What would all these people think if they heard me doing a piddling little six-man football game that nobody cared about? My reputation as a local big-shot would be ruined. I decided not to identify myself on the air.

As the day of the game approached I became more and more nervous. The only play-by-play I had ever tried was into an imaginary microphone in my own room. What if I fluffed? What if I got mike-fright? What if I lost my voice?

There was more at stake than had immediately met my eye. This was the end of the football season, and basketball was right around the corner. Doing basketball would be as easy for me as falling out of bed. Maybe, I thought, Bill Grove wanted to hear how I sounded on play-by-play. If I did a good job on this little six-man game, he might assign some basketball to me. And if I was lousy, he'd write me off as another young fellow who tried to make it in radio and failed.

I went over to St. Mary's, got the names and positions of all the kids on both teams and memorized them. They didn't have any numbers, but at least I would know the backs, who were most likely to carry the ball, and the linemen, who were most likely to make the tackles. Then I went to the field, which was really not much more than a vacant lot, and tried to judge distances from the two goal posts, since there weren't any yard lines.

The day of the game dawned bitter cold. It was late November, and the thermometer was down around zero. The Wyoming winters are pretty grim, and this was a typical winter's day. Just stepping outside was a chore, and I knew that broadcasting a football game from an open field with no shelter of any kind might be a real ordeal.

My back, although much better than it had been, was still painful, and my mother was scared to death I'd get chilled. She made sure I had on woolen underwear and heavy socks and plenty of warm clothes. She fed me a big lunch, with lots of soup and hot coffee, and warned me to be sure and come home if I couldn't stand the cold.

"I don't care if it is your first play-by-play broadcast," she said. "Your back is more important than any football game, and I want you to quit if it's too much for you."

She wished me luck and said she'd listen to every word, even though she didn't know or care much about football. Then, after she promised to send Margaret over with a thermos of hot soup between the halves, I went off to the first radio assignment of my very own. It wasn't much, but it was good for a starter.

At the field I met my broadcasting partner, Dick Lane. He was there to do those five-minute commercials the KFBC salesman had peddled, to act as engineer, cue me in, and help with the color. A stolid, matter-of-fact veteran of several years of radio work, he took this assignment in stride, which was more than I could do.

I kept clearing my throat and taking deep breaths and practicing phrases like, "Jones starts wide to his right—", "Smith moves back to pass—", and "White hits the middle of the line—". There wasn't much Dick could do except tell me not to be nervous.

"Don't worry, Curt," he said. "The mike won't bite you. Anyhow, not very many people will be listening."

My mother would be listening. And I suspected Bill Grove would be listening, too. That was enough for me.

We set things up at midfield, using soap boxes for tables and chairs. I sat on one, Dick sat on another, and we put the amplifier on a third. Then we set up a couple of mikes on collapsible stands, Dick plugged them into the amplifier, and we were ready to go.

Between the cold and the nervousness, my teeth were chattering and there were chills as well as aches in my back. The kids came out to the field and, to my horror, I couldn't tell one from the other. I had to wait until they lined up before I could figure out generally who was who. With no numbers on their backs and no markings on the field this was going to be a great big guessing game. There were no stands either, and only about fifteen spectators. They must have been relatives of the ballplayers. Nobody else would come out to watch a couple of six-man teams fight a battle of what-of-it on a day like that.

Just before we went on the air, I said, "Dick, when you introduce me, don't call me by name. Just say, 'Here's your announcer.'"

"What's the matter?" he asked. "Don't you like publicity?"

"Not if I'm lousy," I said. "And I may be."

"What if you're not lousy?" he said.

"Just don't mention me by name—O.K.?" I said.

The first time he said, "Here's your announcer," I almost choked with fright. St. Mary's was getting ready to kick off, and my voice cracked as I announced that fact. But then the game began, and pretty soon I was talking in conversational tones, just as if I were sitting in my room at the house, talking into my imaginary mike.

I hoped for the impossible—that the teams would stay within sight, between what would have been the forty-yard lines, if there had been any lines. They didn't, of course. Six-man football was apt to be a high-scoring game because there weren't so many tacklers, and this one was no exception. The offensive team was nearly always moving down the field, which meant away from me. When play got near the goal lines, I didn't have any idea who was carrying the ball, where he was going, or how far.

I didn't have time to stay nervous. I was too busy trying to figure out what was going on, and making sure I had the right team in possession of the ball, so I wouldn't use the wrong names. On the air, I spread the glory around pretty thin, naming first one back, then another as the ball-carrier. I kept track of the touchdowns by watching the offensive team. Whenever somebody scored, the boys jumped happily up and down.

Every so often Dick poked me and I said, "And now a word from our sponsors." Then he'd come in with the commercial. We tried to synchronize the commercials with the time-outs, but there weren't enough of those, so we just had to cut in during the game. When I got the mike back I picked up the play where I had left off.

At halftime Margaret came with the thermos bottle of soup, and I wolfed it down. It was so cold my breath looked as if I were smoking, but I can't say I was really uncomfortable. The excitement of broadcasting the game, and the concentration of trying to figure what was happening kept me too busy to worry about the weather.

Before we went back on the air I asked Dick how I sounded.

"I don't know about out there," he said, "but you sounded

fine from here. Are you sure you don't want me to use your name when I introduce you?"

"I'm sure," I said. "If my buddies ever knew I was doing a six-man football game I'd never hear the last of it."

We sailed through the rest of the game without any hitches, except that the weather got worse. I could feel the freezing cold in my bones before the game was over. I didn't know what it might be doing to my back—if anything —but I wouldn't have quit for a million dollars. Six-man football or no six-man football, this was the big test of my life. If I passed it, basketball would be next, and I couldn't have passed it by walking out on it.

I don't remember the final score, or even who won, but I can still see myself sitting on that soap box with Dick at the middle of an unlined field trying to identify unmarked players in a little high school game that didn't mean very much to anybody except the kids and the fifteen people who were there.

I've done World Series and Olympics and football Bowl games in the years since. I've done events that drew over one hundred thousand people in the stands and attracted millions of listeners or television viewers. I've been all over the world and described many different sport spectacles.

I never see a big crowd without thinking of the fifteen hardy souls who went out on a cold November day in 1943 to watch St. Mary's of Cheyenne play Pine Bluffs High School for the six-man football championship of eastern Wyoming. I never walk into a comfortable, heated booth without thinking of the soap boxes at midfield in the freezing playground four blocks from my house. I never look at the complicated piece of machinery which is a modern amplifier without thinking of the portable one we set up on one of those soap boxes. I never pick up a thin, sensitive microphone without thinking of the octagonal mike on a collapsible stand which I used on the day of my first play-by-play broadcast. I never see a messenger bringing a hot lunch to a booth between the halves without thinking of my little sister Margaret delivering the thermos of soup my mother promised. Every engineer reminds me of Dick, and although I haven't seen him for years I think of him whenever I do a commercial or hear somebody else do one.

I was ashamed to be introduced by name, but I'll never forget that six-man football game in Wyoming.

I wonder what I was ashamed of.

4

Although he operated a small station in a limited area, Bill Grove was one of the best all-round radio men I ever met. He knew all phases of the business and could handle practically any chore. One of the few things he couldn't do was announce, but he was a good judge of announcing and had a thorough understanding of what the job required. Without actually being a voice coach, he could help an inexperienced broadcaster with valuable tips.

He was also a crack salesman and a great idea man, who was always dreaming up special projects. A firm, fair boss, he asked nothing more from those who worked for him than what he was willing to do himself. Nobody could keep up with him anyhow. He knew everyone in town, from the governor down, belonged to every service club, and missed very few public functions. The *Eagle,* which was the majority owner of KFBC, recognized Bill's talents, and let him run the station as he pleased.

Bill was a mechanical genius, who could transform a broken-down piece of rusty equipment into a smooth-functioning machine. As an improviser he was in a class by himself. He built a mobile unit for the station out of odds and ends he had picked up, enabling KFBC to get immediately to the scene of news stories and broadcast details on the spot.

He stayed in Cheyenne because he loved the town and the job, and he owned part of the station. I don't know how many lush offers from big companies in Denver he received. He could have made a fortune as an engineer alone. But Cheyenne satisfied all his requirements, and he couldn't understand why anyone would want to leave it.

He had heard part of my six-man football broadcast on his automobile radio, and he told me after returning from a weekend trip that he thought I had promise as a play-by-play announcer.

"You've got a relaxed delivery," he said, "and you know sports. These are the basic ingredients for success in this business, but you still have a lot to learn."

"Like what?" I asked.

"Like not dropping your g's," he said. "And not slurring your words. And not swallowing your sentences. And not lapsing into sing-song tones that might put your listeners to sleep. You didn't do any commercials, but I suspect you'll have trouble with them."

"I thought you said I had the basic ingredients for success," I said.

"I did," Bill said. "You *have* the basic ingredients. What you need are the refinements, and I think you'll learn them as you go along. Now how would you like to do the basketball play-by-play this winter? I'm going to need somebody for that job."

It wasn't long before Bill needed more than a basketball announcer. His staff had already been depleted by the draft, and more men were called after I went to work. Pretty soon I was on a regular eight-hour shift, with sports announcing only part of my duties. More often than not, the engineer and I were the only people in the whole studio.

I learned the broadcasting business from the ground up during those wartime years. I did news, station breaks, commercials, and interviews. I cued in national shows and I spun records. I covered fires, robberies, shootings, speeches, and kaffee klatches.

But no matter what else was happening, I always managed to give sports priority. The local games came first, and sometimes I could wangle a trip to Laramie for Wyoming games. Bill went almost everywhere with me, for he was an ardent sports fan himself. He took over as engineer on the mobile unit because he couldn't spare a regular engineer from the studio.

I also continued to write for the *Eagle*, which was just as short-handed as the station. Eventually, I became the sports editor, which meant doing a daily column and supervising a small staff. There weren't any conflicts because I covered the games I announced. The two jobs dovetailed very nicely.

But I liked radio work much better, because I preferred talking to writing and felt that I was better at it. Besides, Bill constantly talked radio to me, for he was completely sold on it as a future for any young fellow with an adequate voice and a willingness to learn. He became more than a boss, for he was also a good friend and a valued adviser.

Yet he nearly fired me once, and I wouldn't have blamed him if he had.

I was working a 3 to 11 P.M. shift at the station and spending the mornings at the paper. One day I ran into a friend named Al Weppner, who loved to fly-fish a little stream called Horse Creek, about forty miles from Cheyenne.

"Hey, Curt," he said, "the trout are really hitting there. Let's take a ride up."

"I have to be at the studio at three," I said.

"It's only eleven now," he said. "We can drive up, stay a couple of hours, and get back in plenty of time. Curt, you ought to see those fish—eight or nine inches, perfect for eating, and just standing in line to be caught."

By then I was practically drooling, and Al didn't have to twist my arm to get me into his car. All the way up he kept telling me not to worry, that he'd get me back by three no matter how good the fishing was or how much we'd be tempted to stay. After we arrived we couldn't get out of the car fast enough.

Weppner hadn't exaggerated one bit. We used little dry

flies and plucked those beautiful eating trout out of the
water almost as fast as we got our lines in, and pretty
soon I lost all track of time.

The next thing I knew it was five in the afternoon.
"I can't quit now," I said. "What the heck, somebody
else will cover for me anyhow."

So we stayed around Horse Creek until dark and it was
nine or ten that night before we were back in Cheyenne.
I didn't even bother to call the station.

The phone woke me up the next morning. It was Bill.
"Are you coming downtown today?" he asked. "If you
do, will you honor us with a visit? I'd like to talk to you."

When I arrived he said, "Curt, you've been doing a great
job here. You've pitched in and helped us in all sorts of
ways, and you've been particularly good on sports. If you
work hard I think you can go places because you've got a
lot of natural ability. You have a nice manner with people,
and you're a good guy to travel with. I like you personally
and I've enjoyed our trips together.

"Yesterday you did something I never thought you were
capable of. You just took off without a word to anyone.
You didn't call in advance and you didn't call later. You
stuck another fellow with an eight-hour shift he didn't expect and shouldn't have had to take. You know he has a
wife and three children, and he couldn't even tell her if
he'd be home for supper.

"Curt," he said, "I want to know—right now. Are you
going to work here or aren't you? If you're going to work
you'll live by my rules. If you don't intend to live by my
rules, you're fired. You've got about three seconds to make
up your mind."

I apologized. Then I called the guy who had filled in
for me and apologized to him and arranged to make up the
time he had put in for me.

From that day to this, the only thing that ever stopped
me from being where I was supposed to be when I was

supposed to be there was illness. When I was too sick to show up I phoned in or had somebody do it for me.

Bill and I were actually closer after the incident than we had been before. I appreciated the job more because I had nearly lost it, and he said he appreciated my being there more because he had come so close to firing me. As a matter of fact, he was so short-handed already that he would have had trouble finding a replacement. But he hadn't hesitated to let me know I was through if I didn't obey his rules and I respected him for it.

He continued to keep after me to improve my delivery. I think most sports announcers have a tendency to lapse into a sing-song voice, especially when broadcasting basketball. The action is fast and the scoring frequent, so there's bound to be a certain amount of repetition. It can also happen in football, where backfields are always going into the same formations on offense. It's less likely to happen in baseball, which has periods of inactivity that require the announcer to use his ingenuity in filling in the dead spots.

I guess this was my biggest fault when I first started announcing. Time and again Bill would say, "Curt, you're getting sing-song," right in the middle of a broadcast. And later he would tell me, "You've got to let your voice drop at the end of a sentence—that's the announcer's only way of putting a period in his voice. When you keep to the same pitch all the time you sing-song."

It took me a long time to get over the habit. And it took me a longer time to read commercials properly.

"You're not just an announcer when you read commercials," Bill said. "You're a salesman. You're telling the public to buy something, but if you don't sound as if you'd buy it yourself you won't get anybody else to buy it. No matter how you *felt*, you have to *sound* sincere."

"But some of these commercials are ridiculous," I said. "How can I sound sincere when I don't believe what I'm reading?"

"I can tell by your voice when you think a commercial is ridiculous," he said. "You talk as if it's a necessary evil. Maybe it is, but it's the stuff that keeps radio stations alive. If you don't learn to read commercials right you'll always be under a handicap getting a job. No sponsor will hire you if you sound as if it's a chore to pitch his product. Don't forget, he's the fellow who pays your salary. You must give him the best you've got."

We talked about this time and again, but I still couldn't make a commercial sound convincing. Patience was one of Bill's greatest virtues and he never got upset at my repeated failures to improve.

"You'll learn," he said. "Some day it'll come to you. You'll pick up a piece of paper and read the commercial that's written on it exactly as it should be read. It will happen suddenly and you won't need me to tell you it's happened. You'll realize that yourself. You will sound like you were talking to a friend across the kitchen table, not like an orator."

And it finally did happen, just as Bill said it would, over a year after I started working at KFBC. We were broadcasting a high school basketball game, sponsored by several merchants in town. I picked up one of the commercials—I think it was for a men's shop—and started reading it with the same enthusiasm I had in announcing the game. It sounded right, and I knew it sounded right. And later Bill Grove said, "You've got it, Curt. I knew you'd do it sooner or later."

Commercials came easier after that. But to this day I can't do one well without thoroughly believing in the product I'm trying to sell. As a matter of fact, if I can't believe in it enough to use it myself I won't even try to pitch it. I've turned down contracts rather than accept a sponsor I wasn't sold on.

Our quietest sports period in Cheyenne was the summer. We had no local baseball after school was out, and there wasn't enough interest in the Denver ball club to go there and do their games live. But Bill knew we could sell big league baseball if we could get it, and one day he said, "Do you think you could re-create games if we got the play-by-play by wire direct from the ball park?"

My heart missed a beat or two. Imagine me, a guy who hadn't seen a dozen major league games in his life, actually broadcasting them!

"I'd sure like to try," I said.

It took Bill a day or two to round up enough sponsors among the local business people, and the next thing I knew I was sitting in the studio telling our KFBC audience all about the game we had picked for that day.

I had heard re-creations of games while I was in the service back East, but had never seen one actually done. There really wasn't much to it. The announcer sat beside a Western Union operator who received the play-by-play direct from the ball park in the briefest form—1B for a ball, 1S for a strike, 2B, 2S, etc. Batters were given by name, and fielding plays by numbers that are standard in baseball scoring, 1 for the pitcher, 2 for the catcher, 3 for the first baseman, up to the right fielder, who is 9. Thus, if the ticker said a play went 5–3, for example, it meant the third baseman fielded the ball and threw the batter out at first.

All this was easy for me to understand, as it would be for any hot baseball fan. Of all the broadcasting jobs I ever did in Cheyenne, re-creating ball games gave me the biggest thrill. Bill let me pick the game I wanted to do, the operator would contact the park where it was played, and for about three hours every day I was a big league baseball announcer.

I got pictures of all the ball parks, and propped up the right one in front of me so I'd know the layout of the place I was talking about. Pretty soon I had all the dimensions memorized, and I could tell at a glance if a home run, for instance, was hit into stands or over a fence. I had a couple of record books, and clipped the latest statistics from the paper every day.

The wire services gave us odd bits of information—the weather, the size of the crowd, the warmup pitchers, and other useful dope that could help an announcer two thousand miles away set the stage before the game. We had a recording of crowd noises of different intensity which I could turn on and off at will, depending on the attendance and the game situation. I also had a stick and a little block of wood for simulating hits. If the batter fouled one off or barely got a piece of the ball, I'd hit the block a glancing blow; if he hit a line drive or a long smash, I'd give it a solid belt.

I learned years later that many announcers dislike re-creations because there are so many dead spots to fill, but I loved them. I gobbled up every scrap of baseball information I could get from newspapers, record books, and magazines, then used the material on the air whenever the occasion arose. Of course, all I knew was what I read, for I had never met a big league ballplayer in my life except to ask for autographs. But now I felt as though I were part of baseball, for every day I was describing a game actually in progress. It was the next best thing to being there.

Another thing I liked about re-creation was that there was nearly always a big league game somewhere, especially during the last half of the season when open dates were used to make up previous rainouts. If the game we planned to broadcast was postponed, we just switched somewhere else. I never got sick of the games—in fact, I couldn't get enough of them. Doubleheaders put me in seventh heaven; blank days left me desolate.

Re-creating gave me an advantage over announcers on the spot because I knew what was going to happen and they didn't. I always kept at least half an inning behind the action, so I could set up in my mind exactly how to handle it. This also helped me avoid mistakes. With everything right in front of me I couldn't go wrong.

It's much easier to re-create a game than to do one live. Although you must ad lib a great deal, you don't have to think nearly as fast. Almost any game produces a few complicated plays which the live broadcaster must call as he sees. By the time the studio broadcaster gets it, it's all done up in a neat little package for him.

On the other hand, ad libbing can be a problem in re-creating a ball game. I doubt if ad libbing can really be taught. The gift of gab is something a person is born with. It takes a non-stop tongue, a good deal of information, a fair amount of imagination, and plenty of nerve. Any time an announcer sits down to re-create a ball game he knows he's going to have to do a tremendous amount of extra-curricular talking. Air time is valuable and not one minute of it can be wasted.

As always, my mother was my severest critic. A perfectionist in the use of English, she had something to say about every one of my broadcasts. When I arrived home she had half a dozen corrections neatly noted down, and the first thing she did was hand them to me.

"Today," she would say, "you mispronounced five words and used poor grammar seven times. And you're slurring again. Talk a little slower."

Each mispronounced word and each grammatical error would be written down twice—the way I said it and the way it should be said. Then my mother would make me repeat the correct version until I got it right. If it were a mistake I had made before, she reminded me of that fact and told me to be more careful in the future.

Of course I didn't like it. Anything Bill Grove told me I accepted without question, but it irritated me to hear the same things from my mother. She knew it, but she kept right on correcting me. And, whether I liked it or not, I tried to do as she said.

"Some day," I once said to her, "I'll come home and you won't have anything to criticize."

"It will never happen," she said.

It never did. It hasn't happened yet. Hard as I try not to, I still mispronounce a word here and there, still use poor grammatical construction occasionally, and still sometimes slur words and phrases.

I spent two years with Bill Grove, the two most critical years of my career, for everything I did later rested on the combination of what he taught me and what I learned from experience at his radio station. Most of those two years I worked within a radius of twenty-five miles of Cheyenne, but there were some longer trips that I never forgot.

One was to Chicago to follow the Fort Warren basketball team. Bill sold the time we needed to make the trip worthwhile, and the two of us traveled first class all the way. Another was to Denver for the National A.A.U. basketball tournament. We nearly missed that one because we were one sponsor short right up to the last minute.

There were two Greek restaurants, the Mayflower and the Valencia, right across the street from each other not far from the studio. On the day before we were supposed to leave town, Bill and I walked into the Mayflower and talked to Gus Andraws, one of the owners.

"Room for one more, that's all," Bill said, after explaining our deal.

"I don't want it," Gus said. "Who cares about the National A.A.U. tournament?"

"A lot of people care," Bill said. "Look at all the sponsors we have already."

"Then you don't need me," Gus said. "Anyhow, we've got enough things on the station."

"Well, all right," Bill said. "I guess we'll have to go over to the Valencia."

Gus frowned. "You mean if I don't buy it you'll give them a chance?" he asked.

"Sure," Bill said. "I told you there's room for only one more."

"O.K., O.K.," Gus said. "Put me down."

So we put him down and went to Denver the next day to cover the tournament.

In August of 1945, just after the war ended, I had a phone call from a man named Kenyon Brown.

"I run KOMA in Oklahoma City," he said. "We're a fifty-thousand-watt C.B.S. station. I've heard about you and I'd like to talk with you. Come and see me at the Plains Hotel. Bring a scrapbook and a few of your records."

The call thrilled and mystified me. How would the boss of a big station in Oklahoma City ever have heard of a green announcer in an isolated town the size of Cheyenne? And what in the world would make him interested in me?

The answers lay in a combination of circumstances, one sheer accident, the other sheer coincidence. While driving along Route 30, the Lincoln Highway, which runs through Cheyenne, Mr. Brown turned on his automobile radio and happened to catch me doing a baseball re-creation. He planned to stop in Cheyenne to see a cousin there named Rod Hertel, and that was where the coincidence came in. Rod Hertel worked in the same Union Pacific Railroad office as my father, and the two often listened to my broadcasts together.

Having heard me on the air, Mr. Brown asked his cousin about me. I guess Rod didn't exactly give me the worst of it. The phone call was the result and, needless to say, I got down to the Plains Hotel as fast as I could.

Mr. Brown looked at the material I brought and listened to my records. Then we talked at considerable length. I must have bored him to death with questions about big-time broadcasting, but he answered them all with clarity and patience. He told me that he thought the end of the war would be followed by the greatest sports boom in history, for millions of Americans would turn to sports as one of their most important entertainment outlets.

"We thought sports broadcasting was big before the war," he said. "It was small compared to what it will be now, because it's going to blossom into a major industry."

He didn't offer me a job, but he told me I'd hear from him in the near future, and I floated out of there on a big rosy cloud. I wasn't counting any chickens, but Mr. Brown's interest was certainly more than casual. Obviously, he had something in mind for me.

Around that time, I was busy on a project in connection with my job as sports editor of the *Eagle*. With the end of the war, *Esquire* Magazine was sponsoring an All-American boys East-West baseball game at the Polo Grounds in New York. Selected sports editors around the country were asked to pick the best young ballplayers in their regions, and I had been chosen to find one in the Wyoming-Montana area.

This, too, was a thrilling experience for me, since I would take the player to New York, where we would meet and mingle with the nation's leading sports writers and columnists. Of all the trips I had ever made, I looked forward to this one the most.

The boy I selected was a seventeen-year-old infielder from Helena, Montana, named Herb Plews, who later played for some years for the old Washington Senators. We were to meet in Denver, and go east from there, along with Chet Nelson, the sports editor of Denver's *Rocky Mountain News*, and the Colorado ballplayer Nelson had selected.

Two days before I left I had another call from Kenyon Brown, this time from Oklahoma City.

"I need a sports director for KOMA," he said. "The job is yours if you want it."

He named a salary far beyond what I was making in two jobs in Cheyenne. I would do the University of Oklahoma football games, run a couple of sports programs every day, and handle sports in general in the area.

At first the whole thing seemed almost more than I could grasp. For me, Oklahoma City was the big time, and I wondered if I could make it there. It was one thing to talk to Mr. Brown in the Plains Hotel and hope he might offer me a job. It was quite another actually to receive the offer and be faced with the certainty of permanently forsaking the only home I had ever known in a town I truly loved.

For even as I spoke with Mr. Brown I felt pangs of impending regret at the thought of leaving Cheyenne. I was comfortable and contented there. I didn't make much money, but it was adequate for my needs. I had two nice jobs, a wonderful boss, and my choice of a hundred little streams to fish. My family was there and so were my closest friends.

And there was my back to think about. It had continued to improve, but it would always be weak and I never knew what might happen to it. If anything went wrong with it in Cheyenne I didn't have to worry about my job because Bill Grove knew about it and would always hold the job open for me. But what if something went wrong in Oklahoma City? Where would I be then?

I thanked Mr. Brown and asked if I could wait until my return from New York before giving him an answer. He told me to take my time and that he understood my doubts. He added that if he hadn't been sure I could handle the job he wouldn't have offered it to me.

Both my parents were as thrilled as I over the offer and, even though it meant leaving home, they urged me to take it.

"If radio work is going to be your career, you can't stay here forever," my mother said. "Oklahoma City is much bigger than Cheyenne, and there are places around the country much bigger than Oklahoma City. This is a natural move for you, and when you have a chance to advance beyond there, that will be another natural move."

Bill Grove wasn't so sure. Our own football season was coming, and he thought I should stay in Cheyenne at least until it was over. At his suggestion, I talked with Tracy McCracken, publisher of the Cheyenne papers and principal owner of the radio station.

"I don't think you should go, Curt," he said. "You're doing well here, but that doesn't mean you'd do well in Oklahoma City. A sports announcer is like a fighter. He may be a champion in his own weight division, but if he tries to go beyond it he finds himself overmatched and outclassed. I don't think you're quite ready for that big market and that big station down there."

Tracy McCracken, a self-made man, is gone now, but he was one of the brightest men I have ever met. When he gave you advice, it was well worth heeding. I was inclined to agree with him, but how would I or anyone ever know I was outclassed unless I took a crack at something bigger than Cheyenne?

But I wasn't quite sure. I had those nagging doubts, and they wouldn't leave me. They were still with me when I went to Denver for the train trip east with Chet Nelson and the two young ballplayers.

I had four wonderful days in New York. We stayed at the New Yorker Hotel, where we met at five or six every evening—sports editors and columnists from all over America and me, an unknown from Cheyenne, Wyoming. We went on radio broadcasts, and talked to ballplayers and hobnobbed with the great and near-great. I met Babe Ruth, who was manager of the East team, and Ty Cobb, who managed the West. I met O. B. Keeler from Atlanta, and Royal Brougham from Seattle, and Braven Dyer from Los Angeles, and Bill Leiser from San Francisco, and dozens of other prominent sports figures. I met Grantland Rice and Lawton Carver and Frank Graham and many of the other big-time New York writers, and nothing gave me a bigger kick than to sit around and listen until three or four in the morning while those fellows who had just been names to me before swapped stories right in the same room with me.

We all traveled around together and talked and became good friends, and after a while I decided to tell them about my offer and ask them what I should do. To a man, they told me to take it; not one of those writers told me to turn it down.

I remember Granny Rice saying, "Look, you're a young fellow, just starting out. The only way for you to go is up. If you're on a small newspaper you move to a bigger one, and the same thing is true of a radio station. This might be your only chance. Don't pass it up."

I didn't even wait to get home. I called Bill Grove from New York and told him I was going to Oklahoma City. Then I phoned Kenyon Brown and accepted his offer.

Oklahoma City wasn't the big leagues, but it was a lot closer than Cheyenne.

I was on my way.

5

The only person in the whole state of Oklahoma I knew was Kenyon Brown, and I didn't know him very well. I arrived in Oklahoma City by plane late one night and checked into the Biltmore Hotel, where the KOMA studios were. The next day I walked into the station and the receptionist took me into Mr. Brown's office. He greeted me like a long-lost brother.

"Sit down and relax, Curt, while I tell you about this job," he said. "There'll be lots of opportunities and we're always open for new ideas, so don't ever be afraid to suggest anything. I want you to go over to Norman in our station wagon and meet the Oklahoma football coaches and the boys on the team. You're going to see a lot of those people because you'll broadcast their games live wherever they're played.

"You'll also do two daily sports shows, one at five-fifteen in the afternoon, the other at ten-fifteen at night," he went on. "But you won't have to worry about those for a few days. Get settled, learn your way around town, and make yourself at home."

"I'm ready to work right now, Mr. Brown," I said.

"The name's Ken," he said. "Go on over to Norman this afternoon if you want to."

He introduced me around the studio, and everybody gave me such a big welcome that Cheyenne seemed a lot farther back in time than twenty-four hours. One of the KOMA announcers, a fellow named Ben Holmes who was about my age, had an apartment and was looking for a roommate. I moved in with him and he was one of my closest friends all the time I was in Oklahoma City.

That afternoon I drove to Norman, about thirty miles away, and went first to see Harold Keith, the Oklahoma sports publicity director. Keith showed me all over the university's sports plant, and introduced me to Dewey (Snorter) Luster, the football coach, and the boys on his staff and on the team. My first football broadcast was the Oklahoma-Hondo Air Base game, which opened the Sooners' season. Oklahoma's next game, against Nebraska at Lincoln, was very nearly my last.

I drove up with Tommy Thomas, the chief engineer at KOMA, and Bill Bryan, the program director. Long trips were tough on my back, which stiffened up when I sat in one position too long. The only way I could find relief was by lying flat in the back of the station wagon. I did that on the way to Lincoln the day before the game, and again on the way back the day after.

It was a beautiful clear Sunday morning when we left Lincoln, with Tommy driving, Bill on the front seat beside him, and me stretched out in back. We had been traveling about three hours, and were moving at a pretty good clip somewhere in Kansas when I heard Tommy say, "Look at that guy. He must be drunk or something."

I propped myself up and looked down the road. An ancient Model A Ford, still a good distance away, was chugging along on our side of the highway, headed right for us. With nothing else coming the other way, Tommy swung over to pass him on the left.

Just then, the driver of the old rattletrap woke up to the fact that he wasn't where he belonged and he moved over to the other lane, so again we were headed right for each other. Now there wasn't time for Tommy to get back to our side of the road and we met head on. Something hit me with tremendous force and the last thing I remember was a fleeting thought that we were all going to be killed.

I couldn't have been unconscious very long because I was still in the back of the wagon when I came to. My shoulder felt as if it were on fire and so did my back, and there was blood all over me. Neither the shoulder nor the blood scared me because all I could think of was my back. One of my worries about leaving Cheyenne had been the possibility of losing my job if anything happened to it, and now something obviously had.

I heard moaning in the front seat and somebody mumbling that the other guy should have stayed on his own side of the road, so I knew that Tommy and Bill were alive at least. As it turned out, except for whatever effect this had on my back, nobody was very badly hurt. I had a dislocated shoulder and a broken nose, Bill had a deep cut on his face and a brain concussion, and Tommy broke a knee-cap.

Ken Brown came up to Kansas as soon as he heard about the accident. With some misgivings, because I didn't know how he would take it, I told him the whole story of my back, and my fears that if it kicked up on me and I had to be out for a long time it would cost me my job.

"Don't worry, Curt," he said. "You're not going to lose your job, no matter how long you're laid up. When we get back to Oklahoma City we'll put you into the McBride Clinic. Dr. Earl McBride, who runs it, is one of the best orthopedic surgeons in the Southwest. He'll know what to do about your back."

I spent nearly three weeks at the McBride Clinic. The doctor didn't do anything about my back until the other effects of the accident started wearing off. Then he told me there was a chance the crash had done some good.

"I don't know what we'll have to do eventually," he said, "but it's possible that accident cut some of those adhesions loose. It hurts now, but it might be better in the long run."

It didn't feel any better. I got back on the job before the football season was over, but I didn't do any more moving around than I had to. I used a cane when I walked and was in almost constant pain, with traveling tougher than ever. But I managed to live with it while handling my sports shows and covering the last few football games of the season.

If I learned nothing else from that 1945 season, I learned how little I really knew about football. In Cheyenne I had covered only schoolboy games, and had never had a chance to discuss the fine points of the game with an expert. After the accident there wasn't any chance for me to do it at Oklahoma either. It was all I could do simply to get to the games and report them as I saw them.

Football was my weakest major sport. I knew basketball well, from playing it, discussing it with top-notch coaches, and announcing it. Although I didn't know any big league ballplayers or managers, I was pretty good on baseball after all those re-creations in Cheyenne. But inside football was a mystery to me. The game is very scientific and I could learn its angles only by study and discussion with the men who knew them.

Oklahoma had only a fair season in 1945—won five games and lost five—and Snorter Luster was replaced by Jim Tatum, who had built up a great record as a coach of Navy teams during World War II. I hoped that when my back was all right again I could get to know Tatum, or at least somebody on his staff, well enough to learn the things about the game I felt any competent football announcer should know.

In the meantime, the basketball season was beginning, and Oklahoma A. & M. had the best college team in the country. The Aggies had won the national championship the previous year and were favored to win again in the 1945-46 season. The University of Oklahoma also had a good team.

Somewhat to my surprise KOMA wasn't in the habit of

covering basketball on any sort of full-time basis, so I talked to Ken Brown about it.

"This is a great game for excitement," I told him. "And I've played it all my life and covered it regularly in Cheyenne."

"As a fifty-thousand-watt station, we can't afford to give up prime evening network time," he said. "People want the big national programs and we can't substitute local basketball for them."

"But our local basketball *is* of national interest," I said. "Especially A. & M. They're the champions."

He thought about it a few days, then agreed to put the games on at ten-fifteen. This meant I'd have to record them, but that didn't matter; it was just like broadcasting live. And, as it turned out, with that big strong KOMA signal, the games covered a huge area. Late at night even my folks in Cheyenne could hear me.

My first basketball broadcast over KOMA was Oklahoma A. & M.'s second game of the season, against DePaul at Stillwater, Oklahoma. The station engineer drove and I lay in the back of the wagon. The game was a real thriller, featuring a pair of giants, Bob Kurland, A. & M.'s seven-footer, and DePaul's George Mikan, who stood six-ten. It seesawed back and forth, but DePaul finally pulled out a four-point victory.

The Aggies then went on to win thirty of their next thirty-one games. The only other team to beat them was Bowling Green, led by the great six-eleven Don Otten. But the A. & M. boys went on to win their last fifteen in a row, including the semi-finals of the nationals over California and the finals over North Carolina at Madison Square Garden. That gave them their second successive national championship.

Thanks to those delayed broadcasts, which we did all year, the whole southwestern part of the country went mad for Oklahoma A. & M. I traveled everywhere with the team, during which time I became very friendly with Hank Iba, the Aggies' coach, and his family. In the absence of my own folks, the Ibas were like foster parents to me. They often insisted that I stay over with them to save me the night trip back to Oklahoma City, and I must have eaten half my meals with them that season.

I had thought I was a basketball expert until I met Iba. He talked basketball morning, noon, and night, and I learned more from him that winter than I had ever known in all the years I had been associated with the game. He told me basketball was going through a transformation that would be climaxed by the highest-scoring games in history. He foresaw the one-hundred-point scores that have since become commonplace and the day—which has arrived in pro basketball—when men six-five and six-six would be playing in the backcourt instead of up front.

Our A. & M. broadcasts were sponsored by the Oklahoma Gas and Electric Company. After the Aggies won the nationals, which I broadcast back to Oklahoma direct from Madison Square Garden, Ken Brown threw them a big victory dinner. I guess people came from all over the state and perhaps farther, because the affair was an absolute sellout. I was master-of-ceremonies, a labor of love. Up to that time, I had never done much speaking before a live audience, but I enjoyed it and did more and more during my years in Oklahoma City.

That dinner was my last public appearance for a long time because the pains in my back and my legs were driving me out of my mind. All the traveling had aggravated the situation, but I hadn't wanted to miss any of the A. & M. games. I think the excitement of the season helped keep my mind off my troubles, but with basketball over I didn't have anything else to think about.

I knew something would have to be done, but I wasn't sure what, who should do it, or where. Dr. McBride thought I needed a spinal fusion, and I wondered if I ought to go back to the Mayo Clinic, where I had had my first operation. However, I had developed a lot of faith in Dr. McBride, and I finally decided to let him go ahead.

He told me later I had one of the worst cases of adhesions he had ever seen, and that he was sure they were responsible for the terrific pain I'd had since the accident in Kansas. He did the fusion in the lower part of my back, grafting bone from my hip, and told me that he thought I'd be all right eventually. But he warned I'd have a good deal of pain first, and he didn't want me to think about working for at least six months.

Ken Brown said I could stay out as long as I wanted without worrying about the job. "Take the summer off," he said. "And maybe by autumn you'll be able to pick up football again."

I was in the hospital about a month after the operation, and then went home to Cheyenne in May for what turned out to be a long, hot summer. All I could think of was that horrible summer after I got out of the Army, when all I did was gripe about my pains and get into people's way.

But 1946 was even worse. Having had a taste of the big time, I wanted more, and I knew I wouldn't see any in Cheyenne. I missed Oklahoma City and all my friends there, and, despite Ken Brown's assurances, I worried constantly about my job. It was all right for him to promise it would always be there, but suppose I had to stay away for a couple of years? He couldn't keep it on ice for me indefinitely.

Every so often he would call and ask how I was, and I'd have to tell him there was no appreciable change. I was too uncomfortable even to go fishing. I sat around the house most of the time, reading and moping and gulping codeine and wondering if the morning would ever come that I would wake up without pain.

In August I called Ken and said, "I'll be honest with you.

My back and legs are as bad as ever. I don't know whether I'll be able to make the football season or not."

"Look, Curt," he said, "you're not doing yourself any good there. Come on down for a checkup and while you're here we'll talk things over."

So later in the month I went to Oklahoma City and checked back into the McBride Clinic. The doctor put me into a big body brace and told me the only thing that would help me was time.

"And while you're waiting for it to pass," he said, "try to go back to work. If you can stand it, you'll be much better off. There isn't another thing medical science can do for you."

Ken wanted me to try, at least, to keep one of my daily shows going. I got a room at the Biltmore, and spent all my time in it except to take the elevator to the station for the late afternoon show. I got my information mostly by telephone from Harold Keith, and sometimes I'd talk on the phone to Jim Tatum, the new football coach.

But more and more I talked to one of Tatum's young assistants, a fellow not much older than I, whose name was Bud Wilkinson. We had met a few times and sort of gravitated toward each other. I hadn't really had much chance to get acquainted with him, but during that month of September 1946 we talked often together.

The opening game of the season was against Army at West Point. The Army team of that year was one of the greatest in the history of the Academy. The Cadets had such stars as Glenn Davis, Doc Blanchard, Arnold Tucker, and Barney Poole, and everyone expected they would easily win the national championship. They had not lost a game in two seasons, and almost all their victories had been one-sided.

Nobody knew what Oklahoma had. There was not only a new coaching staff, but a whole new team. That was the first year everyone was back from the service, and, with freshmen eligible for varsity competition, it was difficult to judge any of the big college elevens. Tatum brought in some men who had played for him at the Jacksonville Naval Base, so for all I knew Oklahoma was loaded, too.

I would have given anything to make that West Point trip. I wanted to see Blanchard and Davis and that crowd, and I wanted to see what Oklahoma could do against them. But I figured it was just a crazy dream. I had trouble riding from the hotel to the clinic in a car, so how could I hope to ride all the way to West Point in an airplane?

About a week before the game the doctor amazed me by saying, "Curt, I think you should go to the Army game. Ken wants you to cover it and I think it will do you good."

"Every move I make kills me," I said.

"And the longer you wait to make moves the more it will kill you," he said. "Nature and time can do just so much; you've got to do the rest yourself. Your back is definitely better, but you aren't. The longer you sit up there in that hotel room the harder it will be for you to shake yourself loose. Go over to Norman a couple of times this week. Then, no matter how much it hurts, make that West Point trip, and plan to get through the whole football season. You're feeling sorry for yourself instead of fighting this thing."

When I told Ken I'd like a ride to Norman and that the doctor told me to go to West Point later in the week, he laughed.

"I figured the doctor would make you come around," he said. "This will be the best thing that ever happened to you."

I went to Norman the next day and spent a few hours there, talking to Keith and Tatum and Wilkinson and the others. Bud invited me to his home, but that day I had to refuse. I just managed to crawl into the wagon for the painful ride back to Oklahoma City. But later that week I did go over to Bud's, where I met his wife, Mary, and his two boys, Pat and Jay. Both were under ten then. Pat is now on his way to becoming a doctor and Jay graduated from Duke in 1964 after a fine college football career.

Later that fall I spent many an evening with the Wilkinsons. I used to go over there for dinner, and we would have talked football all night if Mary had let us. We became—as we still are—very close friends.

I looked forward to the West Point trip, yet dreaded it. On the day before we took off I tentatively suggested to Ken that perhaps I'd better not go after all, but he wouldn't hear of it. I doped myself up with pills and hobbled onto the plane, wondering if I'd get off alive. The trip itself was a nightmare. I was in agony starting out and I remained in agony all the way.

Ken and the engineer drove me up to West Point from New York the morning of the game, and when we got there I couldn't walk up the stadium steps. They had to carry me to the booth and prop me up in front of the microphone. I guess Ken wasn't sure whether I'd get through the game or not. But when I finally got settled and the teams were ready for the kickoff I felt better, and once the game began I nearly lost myself in it.

It was, for Oklahoma, a fantastic game. Army was a thirty-six-point favorite, but had to fight for its life to win. At halftime the score was 7–7 and everyone, including me, thought we were about to see the upset of the season in the very first game. But Army scored one touchdown on a blocked punt and another when Tucker recovered an Oklahoma fumble on Army's two-yard line with the ball in midair. He then ran ninety-eight yards for the score.

So it ended in a 21–7 victory for Army, but it was the toughest game they had had in three years. Oklahoma's defense was so tight that Davis, for the only time in his brilliant college career, wound up with minus yards gained from scrimmage. From that day on, Oklahoma was a national football power. Everything the Sooners did was watched, and, although they were tripped up a few times, they had a great season. They lost to Texas by a touchdown and to Kansas by three points, but won all their other games, including a lopsided victory over North Carolina State in the Gator Bowl at Jacksonville, Florida.

Ken took me back to New York after the Army game and told me to rest up for a couple of days. I didn't go home until Monday or Tuesday. The trip was rough, but not as bad as the trip east had been. And when I arrived I had to admit my condition had definitely improved.

It continued to as the season progressed. After a while I was able to go to Norman every day, and eventually I could even drive myself there. I broadcast all the football games, both at home and on the road, and by the end of the season I was hooked—as enthusiastic an Oklahoma fan as anyone in town.

We were all thrilled when the boys were invited to the Gator Bowl, thanks to their record of seven victories and three losses against top-flight competition. The Gator Bowl was then just getting started. This was only its second year and it was my first Bowl experience. It wasn't much of a contest, for Oklahoma murdered North Carolina State 34–13, but I never forgot either the game or an incident in Jacksonville the night after it was played.

I went out to dinner alone with Bud Wilkinson that evening. We were talking about the game and discussing football in general when he suddenly asked, "Do you think I'd make a good head coach?"

"I think you'd make a great head coach," I said. "You're sharp and a student of the game and everybody likes you. When the time comes you'll do a fantastic job."

"When the time comes?" Bud said. "How about now?"

I peered at him. He was only thirty and barely nine years out of college.

"Don't you think you're a little young, Bud?" I said. "Some of those service veterans on the team are nearly as old as you. Wouldn't you be afraid they'd try to walk all over you?"

"Not especially," he said. Then, with a half-smile, he added, "Curt, it looks as if Jim Tatum is going to Maryland. Confidentially, they've offered me the job, and I'm going to take it."

"Wonderful!" I said. "I can't imagine anyone I'd rather see get it."

Soon after that conversation Tatum resigned to take the Maryland job, and Wilkinson succeeded him. Although Bud turned thirty-one before the 1947 football season began he was still the youngest coach of a major college team in the country.

As an assistant coach he had helped me a lot. As a head coach he made an expert out of me. Most of the success I've had as a football broadcaster I owe to him. He tutored me as though I were another player, going over formations with me, discussing the jobs of each man in detail, showing me why one maneuver failed and another succeeded, giving me intensive lessons in every phase of the game.

He took me completely into his confidence. I sat with him and his coaches when they reviewed the films of previous games. I was there during skull sessions and special meetings with his quarterbacks. I listened while he explained the weaknesses of the opposition in the game coming up, and I knew exactly how he intended to take advantage of them.

I learned the formations so well that, with Bud's permission, I gave talks on them during the season as a KOMA promotion. Wilkinson was one of the first coaches to use the split T, but he was just as well equipped to use any type of T formation. He taught them all to me from the inside, patiently explaining the different variations and their advantages and disadvantages.

I had an artist draw up big charts, showing the different T formations, then went around the state giving talks

on the subject to civic clubs and service organizations. The
KOMA promotion department booked these talks, so
wherever I went it was explained first that I was there
courtesy of the radio station. The whole state followed
Oklahoma's football fortunes, and some of the people who
heard me were the most rabid fans I've ever seen.

Naturally, they expected the team to do at least as well
under Wilkinson as it had done under Tatum. The boys
won their first two games, so everyone was with Bud in
the early stages of the season. But then Oklahoma took a
34–14 beating by Texas, and after tying Kansas, lost by
two touchdowns to Texas Christian.

Now they had a record of two wins, two losses, and a tie
in their first five games, and that was the end of Bud's
honeymoon. One night during a talk I gave at a country
club in Oklahoma City, a burly fellow got up and said,
"Wilkinson is too young. What does he know about this
game?"

"He's young, but he's a football genius," I said. "Believe
me, Oklahoma's lucky to have him. Give him time and he'll
make history around here."

The critic was backed up by several others, some of
whom demanded why Oklahoma had let Tatum get away.
But Wilkinson had backers there, too, and they helped me
put up a fiery defense of him. The evening almost ended
in a free-for-all because everyone was sore at everyone else,
and they were still arguing when it was time for me to
leave.

Bud heard about it later, and thanked me for raising such
a fuss in his behalf.

"This is my toughest year," he said. "I think we're going
to get all squared away, but these people must be patient.
If they're not, they'll end up demanding an older coach unless fellows like you can keep them under control."

But Bud didn't need any more help from me. The Texas
Christian defeat was his last of the year. His Sooners went

on to win their next five games in a row, and that gave them a better season's record under him than they had had under Tatum.

I spent more time at Bud's home in Norman than in my own apartment in Oklahoma City. One of his assistants was Gomer Jones, who eventually succeeded him as head coach. Gomer used to spend hours at the Wilkinsons' too. Sometimes we'd sit in the kitchen and talk football until Mary made us go home.

Jones loved to cook, so we often went to his apartment. He made the most delicious spaghetti I ever tasted, and was forever throwing parties. But sometimes just Bud and I would go over there, and the three of us would talk football and eat spaghetti until both were practically coming out of our ears.

When the football season ended KOMA switched to basketball. Kurland had graduated, but Oklahoma A. & M. still had a good team, losing only five games all season. Oklahoma also had a good club that winter, so we broadcast their games, too. In case of conflict we took the game that appeared to be the better attraction.

We had also begun doing the Oklahoma City Texas League baseball games in the summer of 1947. The Indians, then a Cleveland Indians' farm club, had two future big league stars in Al Rosen and Ray Boone in 1947 and Boone was around for half the season in 1948, but the team didn't go very far either year. We broadcast the home games live and did re-creations of the road games.

By the summer of 1948 I was a three-sport nut, but busy all the year around. The baseball season ended in Oklahoma City about a week before the football season began, so Ken Brown told me to go home to Cheyenne. I saw the family and did some fishing, and then flew to California, where Oklahoma opened against Santa Clara.

It was a crazy ball game. Oklahoma led, 17–0, at half-time, but Hall Haynes of Santa Clara took complete charge in the second half. He caught three touchdown passes and that gave Santa Clara a 20–17 upset victory. I could hardly believe my eyes, and when I went down to see Bud Wilkinson afterward I found him stunned too.

He was sitting on a stool outside the locker room with his face buried in his hands. When I spoke to him he looked up and, shaking his head, murmured, "We blew it, Curt. We had it in our back pockets and we blew it."

Later, after he had recovered from the shock, he said, "I sure hated to lose this one, but it will be the making of our team. I doubt if we'll lose another ball game all season."

Of course I didn't think he was serious, but I had to admire his confidence. And, being a wild-eyed Oklahoma football fan myself by then, I certainly hoped he was right.

A few weeks later he still hadn't lost another game, and his team was beginning to attract nationwide attention. As the Sooners won victory after victory, the whole Southwest went crazy about them, while the rest of the country watched this young coach and his promising ball club with increasing interest.

Oklahoma's success meant more to me than I realized. One Monday afternoon my phone rang and I had one of the greatest thrills of my life when I heard the voice at the other end. The accent was southern, the tones the most familiar in the sports world at that time.

"Curt, how are you? This is Red Barber in New York."

This is Red Barber in New York. And he was talking personally to me, Curt Gowdy of Oklahoma City via Cheyenne, Wyoming, a local character whom nobody ever heard of outside his own area!

Barber, sports director of the Columbia Broadcasting System, of which KOMA was an affiliate station, was the hottest announcer in the business, the idol of every young sportscaster in America. I had heard him over the air scores of times, and now he was at the other end of my telephone connection, talking to *me*—not the whole nation, but *me*.

If I were to pick the most unforgettable moment of my career, the first greeting over the phone from Red Barber might very well be it.

Somehow or other I managed to stammer a hello.

"Curt," he said, "what looks like the top football game down your way next weekend?"

"Well," I said, "I'd say Oklahoma and Texas Christian." Then my conscience twinged. Maybe I was pushing Oklahoma too hard at the expense of other good teams. As an afterthought I added, "Of course, there's Rice and Texas. That might be as good."

"That's too bad," Barber said. "We were going to put you on that Oklahoma-Texas Christian as the Game of the Week."

I gulped.

"The Game of the Week?" I said. "You mean coast-to-coast?"

"That's right," Red said. "Coast-to-coast. But if you think Rice and Texas might be just as good, maybe we ought to go with that."

"No, Red," I yelled over the phone. "Just wait a minute. This Oklahoma game is going to be great. I didn't want to build it up too much because I was afraid you'd think I was prejudiced."

He laughed, then said, "All right, Curt, you've got the game. We've been planning all along to do Oklahoma-Texas Christian next Saturday."

I was too stunned to say anything. Then I heard that familiar southern voice again.

"Hey, Curt, are you still with me?"

"Sure, I'm with you, Red," I said. "You want me to do the Oklahoma-Texas Christian game coast-to-coast over C.B.S. next week."

The words "coast-to-coast" were magic in those days, as they are to young announcers today. To be on a national network, to know that millions of listeners were within range of my voice, was the ambition of my life, and now for the first time it would be realized. When Red Barber finally wished me luck and hung up, I just sat there shaking. It was hard for me to believe that I had been talking to him directly, let alone that he had asked me to broadcast a major college football game over a national network.

The first thing I did was call Bud Wilkinson.

"We're on C.B.S. next Saturday," I told him.

"Great, Curt!" he said. "I'm happy for you and I'm happy for us. And I hope this will only be the first of a good many times."

Ben Holmes, my roommate and a fine announcer, went over to Norman with me to do the color. Although I had been nervous all week, I woke up that morning composed and confident. On the way over to Norman with Ben I didn't have the slightest qualms about doing the game.

Up in the radio booth that coast-to-coast microphone looked like any other microphone, and as I gazed out to the field it seemed like any other game day. The players looked just the same as ever working out before the game, and that little thrill that comes when the captains meet the officials for the toss just before the kickoff felt the same as it always did.

And, somehow or other, as we began the broadcast, I managed to forget that this was coast-to-coast over C.B.S. and worked as if it were just another Oklahoma football game over station KOMA. So did Ben, who did a remarkable job on the color. The two of us just sat behind our mikes and went to work.

I'm sure Bud felt the same way I did. Even though he knew the whole country was listening to this game, he retained his usual composure and ran his team just as he always ran it. Happily, the result was another Oklahoma victory. I tried to be impartial toward the end. Maybe I sounded that way, but I certainly didn't feel that way. In the last moments of the game I had to fight to control my voice. But the minute it was all over and we had signed off, I gave a whoop of joy and hurried down to congratulate Bud.

Up to then only the Southwest followed the Sooners closely. After that, the whole country was taking a special look at them every week.

Ben and I had hardly walked through the door of our Oklahoma City apartment that night when the receptionist called from the radio station.

"There's a wire here for you, Curt," she said.

"Would you mind reading it to me?" I said.

I heard the crackle of paper as she tore it open. Then she read: "Terrific. Wonderful job on game. My warmest congratulations. Couldn't have been happier. Signed, Red Barber, sports director, C.B.S."

I still have that telegram. A few years later, Red gave me an added thrill by recalling that Ed Murrow had phoned after the game to comment on the excellence of the broadcast.

During the football season, Barber jumped around the country before or after the Game of the Week, depending on the time zone of where it was played. If one happened to be especially interesting he kept it on the air until a quarter ended, then went somewhere else. Otherwise, he moved on after a few minutes.

After the Oklahoma-Texas Christian game, he often cut us into his weekly broadcasts. This, of course, wasn't because of me, but because of Oklahoma. The Sooners kept right on winning. And, just as Bud Wilkinson had predicted after the Santa Clara game, his team ripped through the rest of the season without another defeat.

That was the first year of the most remarkable winning streak in major college football history. Under Wilkinson, Oklahoma went on to win thirty-one straight games over a three-year span. Later, other Wilkinson teams at Oklahoma piled up an even more impressive streak of forty-seven straight victories.

During that 1948 season I was so wrapped up in football, and looking forward so much to the coming basketball season that baseball was tucked far away in the back of my mind.

An unexpected phone call from a casual acquaintance named Jack Slocum suddenly made me the most baseball-minded football announcer in the country.

6

Jack Slocum came from a famous New York writing family. His father, Bill Slocum, had been a baseball writer for years and once was a ghost-writer for Babe Ruth. One of his brothers, Bill, Jr., a former New York *Mirror* columnist, now does a daily column for the New York *Journal-American*. Another brother, Frank, wrote sports for years before joining the staff of the Commissioner of Baseball. Jack himself has been doing publicity, promotion, radio, or television work all his life.

I first met him one night in the summer of 1948 while I was broadcasting a baseball game in Oklahoma City.

We were sponsored by Wheaties, for whom Slocum worked. He had once been radio director of the New York Yankees, and knew the business well. He listened to me, told me he liked my relaxed style, and gave me some valuable tips. Jack was the first professional radio man who ever helped me on baseball.

The football season began soon after he left, and in the excitement of the weeks that followed I had no occasion to think about him. I didn't hear from him again for several months. Then, in mid-November, I had a phone call from New York. It was Jack.

"Curt," he said, "the New York Giants just hired Russ Hodges as their top announcer. That leaves the Yankees' number two job, behind Mel Allen, open. I told Mel and Trevor Adams about you. Adams is the Yankees' radio director. You'll hear from them but that won't mean you've got the job. They're contacting announcers all over the country."

"Thanks, Jack," I said. "I'll be in New York for a basketball game in December."

"Great," he said. "That will give you a chance to meet those guys."

Even before I heard any more, I went to an Oklahoma City public relations guy named Stan Pate.

"I need a brochure about myself," I said. "Will you get one up for me?"

"Sure," he said. "It'll cost you a hundred bucks."

"A hundred bucks?" I exclaimed. "What are you going to make it out of—platinum?"

"It won't be made out of platinum," he said, "but I'll guarantee it will be worth a hundred bucks."

It was, too. Pate made the brochure out of glass, and there wasn't a facet of my career in Oklahoma City that he didn't cover. By judicious use of pictures, newspaper clippings, banquet programs, and everything else he could find that mentioned me, he got out a brochure that made me look like the second coming of Red Barber.

The brochure was all ready by the time I heard from Trevor Adams. He asked me to send a tape from one of my broadcasts and a little information about myself. The tape was my broadcast of the Texas League all-star game that summer. For the little information about myself I enclosed the brochure.

The late Tom Meany, then a highly successful magazine writer, happened to be in the Yankee office when it arrived. He told me later that it was the best job of its kind he had ever seen. And, although both Allen and Adams later insisted it had no effect on their eventual decision, Meany said both spent hours poring over it.

While waiting to hear from New York, I continued my regular work at KOMA. Barber used me from time to time over C.B.S., first on football and then on basketball. He had an evening sports show, and sometimes he cut me in for an interview with Bud Wilkinson, or Hank Iba, or a big league baseball player who lived around Oklahoma City, or some other sports figure.

He asked me to be on the lookout for unusual events, and I kept my eyes open. Once in a while, I'd do something on fishing, or get someone else to. But my prize show for Red was the introduction of the world's championship rattlesnake hunter. He won the title in an annual snake hunt in Oklahoma.

The first I heard about it was through a Sunday feature story in one of the Oklahoma City papers. Barber thought it was a great idea, so I called the man in charge of the hunt. He was delighted.

Then I got cold feet. I'd seen plenty of rattlesnakes in Wyoming, but the thought of being in the same radio studio with a whole lot of them wasn't a happy one. I called the guy back and asked, "Just how do you plan to do this?"

"We'll bring up a few crates of them and get them to rattle while the champion tells how he caught them," he said.

"What kind of crates?" I asked.

"Regular wooden ones," he said. "Don't worry about it. There won't be any danger."

"Are you sure?"

"Positive," he said.

So I told him to come ahead, but I was pretty jumpy and so was everyone else around the station. The only one who didn't mind was the engineer. He worked in a glass booth.

The promoter brought the champion and a couple of crates of the snakes he had caught up to the studio a week or so later. The crates were covered with a canvas top secured by removable clips.

"How do you get them to rattle?" I asked while we were waiting to go on the air.

"We open the tops and poke sticks at them," the champion replied. "That makes them coil up and start rattling."

"How do you know they won't jump out?" I said.

"They can't jump out," he said. "If they try we'll clamp the top back on."

I supposed it was all right, but I wished I were in the glass booth with the engineer.

The champion was a fine talker. He described how to catch a rattlesnake by first trapping it with a noose and a stick, and then grabbing it by the neck and stuffing it into a crate. While he talked he poked away at the snakes and they curled up and went "r-r-r-r-" for the benefit of Red Barber's millions of listeners.

It turned out to be a pretty good show, but I was glad when it ended. The rattling sounded just as ominous in the studio as it had in Wyoming.

A couple of weeks went by and I heard nothing from New York. By then the first thrill of hearing from Slocum and later Adams had worn off, and I realized how little chance I had to get this Yankee job.

A week before Christmas I went to New York with the Oklahoma A. & M. basketball team. I phoned Jack Slocum, and he told me to go to the Yankees' downtown office on Fifth Avenue, that by the time I arrived Trevor Adams would expect me. When I walked into the office, there was Mel Allen, whom I recognized by his picture. I introduced myself to him, and he took me in to see Adams himself.

The first thing they asked me was if I'd ever done any major league baseball. I told them that except for a game at Wrigley Field when I went to Chicago with the Cheyenne softball team, I had never even seen any major league baseball. We talked generally for a while, but neither gave me any indication how they felt about me. When I left I figured I was dead, that they'd surely want someone with more experience than I had.

Back in Oklahoma about three weeks later I had a wire from George Weiss, the Yankees' general manager, asking me to go to New York at their expense for a personal interview. He told me they had narrowed the job down to three men and I was one of the three.

On the train I had plenty of time to get worked up over the situation. Was it possible that the Yankees really might hire me, after all? Were they going to pluck a guy like me out of the obscurity of the Southwest and put him in the New York spotlight?

I thought about my girl—I had finally met the one I wanted to marry—and I wondered how she would like New York. The first time I had seen her was at a national radio and television conference at Norman. The University of Oklahoma had an excellent radio school. If I'm not mistaken it was the first in the country to pay any attention to television, which was in its infancy then.

The conference began with a banquet. I drove alone to Norman, and sat with some fellows I knew, including Sherman Lawton, who was head of the Oklahoma radio school. I happened to glance over at a nearby table, where I saw a beautiful brunette in a black dress and wearing a huge black hat.

"Oh, boy," I said, "isn't she something! Anybody know her?"

"She's one of my students," Professor Lawton said. "Her name is Jerre Dawkins. She's a lovely girl."

"I'll say she's lovely," I said. "I'd like to meet her."

"I'm a professor, not a date bureau," he snapped. "I've told you her name. You'll have to do the rest yourself."

Before going back to Oklahoma City, I found her number in the student directory, and phoned her the next day.

"My name's Curt Gowdy," I said. "I'm a radio announcer in Oklahoma City."

She had never heard of me, which was irritating, since I thought I was pretty well known around there. Furthermore, she wouldn't think of going out with me without first having met me.

It took two weeks of steady calling before she would even

consent to meet me for a Coke in the afternoon. By then
she had made some inquiries about me, and evidently came
to the conclusion that I wasn't a goon. Only after I drove
all the way to Norman just to have a Coke with her did she
agree to a date.

I took her to see a road company starring Joe E. Brown
in *Harvey*, at Oklahoma City. Afterwards, I drove her home
to Edmond, about twelve miles from town, and met her
mother. Later, when Jerre and I began going together, we
spent a good deal of time with Bud and Mary Wilkinson,
both of whom became very fond of her. One evening they
had a party attended by the president of the university. It
was after hours for students, but he didn't know that Jerre
was one. She talked to him a long time, but he never found
out she was one of his co-eds breaking the university curfew.

Jerre graduated that June and spent the summer in Co-
lumbus, Ohio, where she had a vacation job in a radio station. When she returned home we continued to go together,
but had no definite plans to get married.

On the way to meet George Weiss, I decided to get that
situation corrected as soon as I got that Yankee job. Then,
if she were willing, perhaps we could be married in New
York in the spring, since I knew I'd have no chance to go
to Oklahoma City at that time. Every so often, as the train
jolted along, I pulled up short and thought, "Stop dreaming,
Gowdy. You haven't got the job and you're not even sure
of the girl."

I arrived the next morning, and went right from the railroad station to the Yankees' Fifth Avenue office. There, I
talked with Trevor Adams, who told me Allen would be
along any minute. Mel came in at noon and invited me
to lunch, where he said, "Curt, I'd like to have you with me
and I'm pretty sure it will work out that way, but we'll
have to see what happens. George Weiss has the final word,
and I understand you're seeing him this afternoon."

The first thing Weiss asked me was if I thought I'd be happy in New York.

"I'd love it here," I said.

"And how do you feel about working for the Yankees?" he asked.

"It would be the biggest break of my life," I said.

We talked a few minutes, and then I went back to see Trevor. He grinned and said, "Well, Cowboy, how much salary do you want?"

"Don't kid me," I said. "I'm not setting the terms. Whatever you say is all right with me."

I meant it, too. If they had offered me less than I was making in Oklahoma City—which they didn't—I'd have taken the job.

Trevor held out his hand.

"The job's yours, Curt," he said. "Come on over to my apartment and meet my wife. Then we'll go to Toots Shor's for dinner."

So we went to meet Ruth Adams, and I told her all about Jerre and how I wanted her to come to New York. Then we proceeded to Shor's, which has always been a popular gathering place for people in the sports, entertainment, and communications world. It was the first time I set foot in the place.

While I was there I saw Art Flynn and Jack Tanzer, both of whom I had met at baseball games in Oklahoma City. They handled the New York Giants' broadcasts. Before the evening was over, Tanzer cornered me and said, "Curt, we've heard your tapes and like them. You've got a great shot at the Giants' job, working with Russ Hodges. Do you want it?"

I couldn't say yes and I couldn't say no, because the Yankees had pledged me to secrecy. So I stalled him off, and went back to Oklahoma City the next day. A week later the Yankees announced that I was Hodges' replacement as Mel Allen's assistant.

Jerre and I also announced our engagement. We agreed to postpone our marriage until I was all set in my new job. I was to report first to the Yankees' spring training camp in St. Petersburg, Florida, and then go north with them. We could be married in New York during a home stand, which was just what I had hoped while daydreaming on the train.

Besides the new ballplayers, there were two other rookies in the Yankee camp that spring of 1949. I was one. The other was Casey Stengel, who had just been named the manager the previous fall. Stengel, of course, was on a much hotter spot than I. At that time the only thing he was known for was his clowning and his consistent failures as a major league manager. He had previously handled the Brooklyn Dodgers and the Boston Braves, and had never finished in the first division with either.

The old man had plenty of pressure on him right from the beginning. Many observers thought the Yankees had made a mistake in hiring him, and there was some question how the ballplayers would take him. On top of that, Bucky Harris, the man he succeeded, was very popular and, although finishing third, had missed winning the American League pennant in 1948 only by a whisker. Three days before the end of the season the Yankees had been in a triple tie with the Red Sox and the Indians at the top of the league. The Indians finally won in a post-season playoff with the Red Sox.

The day after I arrived in St. Pete, Mr. Weiss had a party for the press, the radio personnel, and all the people in the Yankee organization. Late in the evening I went to the men's room, and there was Stengel. Except for a casual introduction on the field the previous day, this was our first meeting.

"You're one of the radio men, aren't you?" he said.

"Yes, sir," I said.

"I want you to do something for me," Casey said. "There's a fellow on the West Coast who broadcast my games last year who's a great baseball man. He deserves a shot at the big leagues. When we get back to New York, I want you to go to the networks and the agencies and see if we can't get this guy up here where he belongs."

"That's fine, Mr. Stengel," I said. "I think it's wonderful that you're trying to get a break for somebody when you've got so much on your own mind. But this is only my second day in spring training. I'm having a tough enough time making it myself, and I'm in no position to help anybody else. I wish I could. Why don't you talk to Mel Allen?"

"You mean you're new around here, too?" Stengel asked.

"Newer than you are," I said.

He held out his hand and as we shook he said, "Young feller, I hope we both make it."

The man Casey wanted to help was Art Gleeson, who later did come East. He was sports director of the Mutual Broadcasting System at one point. Eventually he became one of our announcers in Boston, a job he held until his sudden death in November of 1964.

Stengel loved to be around young people, and some of the most pleasant hours I spent that year were with him and Frank Scott, our road secretary at the time. After night games Casey would call Scotty and say, "Get Gowdy and come on up." When we arrived, he'd start telling baseball stories, illustrated as only Casey could illustrate.

He had a fantastic memory for names, places, and events. He would begin a story, then take off his coat and tie, and slide across the rug into tables and chairs and divans, never stopping to take a breath. Long before he got to the point, Scotty and I would be rolling around the floor ourselves, for Casey was the funniest man either of us ever knew. While we were still laughing at one story he would launch right into another. More often than not, it was dawn before we went to bed.

One night after we beat the Indians in Cleveland before a crowd of seventy-five thousand fans, Casey got into the back of a crowded hotel elevator and rasped, "What's all the people in town for?"

"There's a ball game with the Yankees," somebody said. "Yeah?" said Casey. "How did it come out?"

"The Yankees won tonight, but the Indians will get 'em."

"You think so, hah?" Casey said. "Lemme tell you something, don't sell them Yankees short. They got a great manager. That Stengel, he's one of the smartest fellers in baseball. You watch, this guy will pull them through. He's very, very smart."

People were muttering and growling and grumbling, but nobody looked back. Casey went all the way to the top and was the last one off the elevator.

Although I met Joe DiMaggio that first spring, I didn't get to see him play at all in Florida. He had had an operation on his heel the year before, and when he reported he was still in pain. He tried to work out, but couldn't do a thing. It looked as if he were through.

The Yankees sent him back up to Johns Hopkins in Baltimore where the operation had been performed, and they told him the only thing that would help was rest. Joe was desolate. All he could do was go to New York and mope. Day after day he just sat around in his hotel room. The only people who saw him were a couple of his closest friends. Each morning the first thing he did after climbing out of bed was test the bad heel. And each morning it hurt so much that he knew he wouldn't be able to play.

This went on all through April and May. Then one morning in June he appeared at Yankee Stadium on an off day, got into a uniform, and took batting practice for an hour or so. Then he got dressed and went out to look for a cab. I was just about to get into one when he came out of the players gate, his face decorated with a huge grin.

"Are you going downtown, Curt?" he yelled.

"Yes," I said. "Come and join me."

His hands were blistered and bleeding. I pointed to them

and asked, "What in the world happened to your hands?"

"Never mind my hands," he said. "That's just from too much batting practice too soon. But my heel—it seems to be all right. I got up this morning and tested it, and there wasn't any pain. Imagine, Curt, for the first time in months —no pain! I threw on my clothes and went down to the lobby and out the door, and walked around the block. No pain. Then I hopped a cab and came out here, and hit for an hour. Still no pain. And no pain now. I think it's all over."

He spent a week getting into shape, and then played a few innings of an exhibition game against the Giants. After that, we flew to Boston for a series with the Red Sox, who were then hot pennant contenders. Every series we played with them was loaded with pressure.

DiMaggio murdered them practically all by himself. His first time up—it was his first appearance in a league game all season—he lined a single to left off Maurice McDermott, the Red Sox left-hander. Later that day he hit a home run. He hit two or three more homers in the series, which the Yankees swept.

In the eighth inning of the last game, right after he belted one over the left-field fence, Stengel let him go to his center-field position. But before play started, Casey pulled him out.

As DiMaggio trotted toward the Yankee dugout the sellout crowd of Boston fans rose and gave him the most tremendous ovation I've ever seen a visiting ballplayer get anywhere. Joe grinned and tipped his cap before disappearing from sight. The cheers continued for several minutes, and he had to stick his head out again before the people would quiet down.

The ovation was a tribute to DiMaggio. The circumstances that triggered it were a tribute to Stengel's flair for the dramatic. Casey had no intention of letting DiMaggio finish the game in center field. The Yankees were well ahead and Joe needed the rest. But if Stengel had simply benched him and sent someone else to center to start the inning there wouldn't have been any ovation.

When I first went to New York I was lonesome and homesick. I missed Jerre terribly, especially after I learned that phone calls were a poor substitute for being with her. At the rate I was making them they cost nearly as much as going to see her would have. And the pace of the big town was a startling change from the free and easy life of Oklahoma City. Living in New York was far different from visiting there. I longed for the days when it was a wide-eyed thrill for me to pop into town and meet all the famous people I had heard of only from a distance. I knew many of them now and liked them, for they were always nice to me. But they had families to go home to, just like everybody else, and all I had to go home to was a room in the Henry Hudson Hotel.

I was also frightened to death of my job. Although I might have been a hotshot in Oklahoma City, I was just another scared young fellow trying to get by in New York. I went there under the impression that I knew the broadcasting business, but I wasn't half the announcer I thought I was. There were refinements to learn, tips to pick up, tricks of the trade to acquire. I knew baseball as a fan; now I had to learn it as an expert. I got plenty of help from Trevor Adams and Mel Allen, but I still had a long way to go before I could call myself a first-class baseball broadcaster.

My hotel was close to Leone's Restaurant which, like Shor's, was a popular hangout for sports figures. Gene Leone was a warm, friendly man with a particularly soft spot in his heart for lonesome young newcomers like me. He understood the pressure I was under and realized how homesick I was.

His place became a second home to me. I ate there regularly, often going in alone late at night for my big meal of the day. Whenever he had a few minutes, Gene came over to keep me company.

"I like to see young fellows come into New York in the entertainment business," he said. "They start just like you—scared and lonely and wishing they were back home. But you know, Curt, after a while they learn that New York is just a great big small town itself. It seems cold, but it really isn't. People are pulling for you and hoping you'll make it. And you will—you've got what it takes."

We talked about my job and the Yankees and basketball and football and my friends back in Oklahoma City. Gene knew Hank Iba, who always went there whenever he took the Oklahoma A. & M. team into New York, and most of the other college basketball coaches were his friends, too. His favorites on the Yankees were the Italian boys—Joe Di-Maggio and Phil Rizzuto and Vic Raschi and Frank Crosetti —but he loved all athletes and anyone who had anything to do with them.

It was nice visiting with people like Gene and being around the ball club, but I knew I'd never be completely happy without Jerre. I couldn't get away from the Yankees long enough to go to Oklahoma to marry her and we didn't want to wait until the baseball season was over, so we decided to get married in New York in June.

Of course I had told Gene Leone about her, and the first place I took her when she arrived in New York was his restaurant. After I introduced her to him I said, "Gene, don't you have private parties in that wine cellar of yours?"

"We sure do," he said.

"Would it be possible for us to reserve that room for our wedding reception?"

"I should say you can, Curt," he said. "How many people do you want to have?"

"About forty," I told him.

"You two have enough to do to get married," Gene said. "My daughter was just married a couple of weeks ago, and

I know exactly what to do. Leave all the details to me."

Jerre was thrilled to have his help and guidance as three days did not give her much time to make arrangements for a wedding, even a simple one.

A few nights later, on the day before an open date, we were married in the beautiful chapel of the Presbyterian Church on Park Avenue. Mel Allen was the best man. We had intended to have only a few close friends attend the ceremony, but somehow I managed to invite about everyone who had any connection with the Yankees, except the players.

Gene had about a thousand candles lighting the wine cellar. There was music, champagne, and a perfect wedding supper. Mr. Leone had even prepared a special ceremony to bring in a huge, beautiful wedding cake.

Harry Grayson, a veteran New York sportswriter whom I didn't know very well at the time, was at the bar when we came in, and recognized the Yankee people. He went over to somebody and asked what was going on.

"Gowdy's having a wedding party in the wine cellar," he was told.

Grayson thought it was Hank Gowdy, the old ballplayer, who had been a good friend of his. As far as he knew, Hank had been happily married for forty years, but if he were about to give it another try Harry wanted to be in on it, so he joined us. Before the evening was over he had stolen the show, for he is one of the most delightful characters I've ever known. We've been close friends from that day to this.

When the party ended, Ruth and Trevor Adams drove us up to Cobb's Mill Inn in Connecticut for our one-day honeymoon. After they left us, Jerre said, "I don't see how you could have been lonesome in New York with all those friends."

Needless to say, I never was again.

Gene Leone, one of the great restauranteurs of the

world, became one of our dearest friends. He went to as much care for our reception as if we had been members of his own family. We shall always remember his wedding gift.

And they say New York is cold!

7

The year 1949 was wonderful for the Yankees and, once I got untracked, wonderful for me. The trouble was, it took me months to get untracked. I went to New York thinking I knew something about broadcasting. Around the time Jerre and I got married I was just beginning to discover the millions of things I didn't know. By then the Yankees, despite an epidemic of injuries that would have discouraged a lesser team and a lesser manager, were well on their way to a winning season. I wasn't so sure about Curt Gowdy.

The tremendous pressure of working in the biggest, most important advertising market in the world scared me. Oklahoma City sponsors spent thousands; New York sponsors spent millions. Oklahoma City sponsors were tolerant of mistakes; New York sponsors, paying for perfection, would settle for nothing less. Oklahoma City sponsors knew there were limits to the returns they might expect; New York sponsors, with such a lush field to draw from, constantly sought expansion. In Oklahoma City competition was hardly a factor; in New York competition was the name of the game.

Whenever I sat behind the microphone at Yankee Stadium I knew there were a dozen fine sports announcers standing in the wings, ready to replace me if I stumbled once too often. I might be permitted a mistake here and there, but I couldn't make many and I'd better not make the same one twice. It would take only a few squawks from those millions of listeners and perhaps only one from a sponsor to send me right back to Oklahoma City—or anywhere else I could get a job.

The pressure was almost a physical thing, a trap waiting to be sprung, a Sword of Damocles hanging over my head. It undermined my confidence, leaving me taut and tense and at times so shaky that I had to drive myself to go on the air at all. My throat went dry and my voice sounded to me more like a croak than the relaxed tones of a professional sports announcer who had knocked them dead in Oklahoma City and Cheyenne. There was many a night in those first few months when I would happily have settled for either.

When I first went to New York I thought I knew all about the Yankees. I soon learned that I had only the knowledge of a rabid fan. I knew who played where, his background, his averages over the years, and anything else about him that had been published, but no more. It was one thing to know the Yankees from the distance of half a continent, but quite another to know them well enough to broadcast their play-by-play to a critical, well-informed audience.

I knew little about major league strategy, the whys and wherefores of moves. I could tell a fast ball from a curve, but I really didn't know very much about pitching. I didn't understand how a pitcher sets up a hitter, why he wastes pitches, what is going through his mind, or what his catcher wants him to do. I had never noticed how fielders played different hitters.

To me, a routine catch of a fly ball in the outfield had always been just that, and no more. I needed an education in why some catches look tough and others easy. I could learn a good deal just from watching Joe DiMaggio play center field. He moved with the hitter, and sometimes with every pitch. He made great catches with such little effort that it seemed anyone could have made them. It took a whole season for me to understand that DiMaggio turned doubles and triples into routine outs.

Mel Allen, my partner and boss, became my teacher as

well. Allen was the hardest-working broadcaster I ever knew. At the time I joined him in New York, he was the hottest sports announcer in the business, but he never let down, never eased off, never missed a detail. He made me pay close attention to everything that happened, not only on the field but in the stands. He had the great faculty of picking up the sidelights that help give a listener the feel of the ball park.

Television was coming fast but hadn't arrived big yet. The broadcaster had to describe everything, and Allen was a master at it. I was anything but, for the only thing I ever had done before was broadcast what was right in front of my nose. Mel taught me to look everywhere in the ball park for material so that I could build a word picture of the baseball atmosphere, not just the game itself.

Until I began working with him, a foul ball was just another strike. But Mel made me follow every foul that went into the stands, to describe the kids going after it or the fan catching it, to let the listening audience in on the crowd reaction.

"The fans are just as much a part of the game as the players," he used to say. "If you ignore them you're not doing your job."

Allen also taught me the fine points of giving commercials. I had learned the fundamentals from Bill Grove in Cheyenne, but I always felt funny giving commercials and had never been very good at it. Those big-spending sponsors didn't want funny-feeling announcers pitching their products to the millions of people who listened to the Yankee broadcasts. They wanted the job done with heart and confidence and sincerity.

I did it all wrong. I recited the commercials like a first-grade lesson. I read them as if every word were an ordeal. I was nervous and sing-songy and about as convincing as a sleepwalker. With Mel pushing me, I practiced at home, then practiced some more at the ball park, trying to develop the same casual style in giving commercials as in describing a game. Believe me, it wasn't easy.

Another thing Allen taught me was how to lead into commercials so that they didn't sound stereotyped and stilted. He was great at this. To the best of my knowledge, he was the first sports announcer to combine commercials with the action on the field.

"Henrich is rounding third base and heading for the plate," he would say. "It's going to be close—he's running —he hits the dirt—he slides—and he's safe! Boy, that sure was close—a tough decision for the umpire. But you don't have a tough decision when it comes to White Owl cigars—"

Then, in the same tone of voice, he'd go into the commercial. He made it as natural as Henrich sliding home.

Although I rarely saw him because he was with the Brooklyn Dodgers, Red Barber became a good friend of mine. The Dodgers were sometimes home when we were, and Red phoned every so often to give me encouragement. He kept telling me not to worry—that I was doing fine and would do better.

When the baseball season ended Red, as sports director of the Columbia Broadcasting System, hired me to do his Football Scoreboard show at six-fifteen on Saturday nights. This was my first regular network job, a fifteen-minute program broadcast from the C.B.S. building on Madison Avenue in New York. John Derr, who was the producer and director, had it written by staff men and we'd check the copy before putting it on the air. I'd give the scores and talk a little about each major game.

We put the show together on the ninth floor and broadcast from one of the studios on the fifteenth floor. It took only a minute or two to get from one place to the other, so I figured I'd be safe leaving the ninth floor at six-ten. About three weeks after the football season began, I left the ninth-floor office and stood at the elevators, waiting for an up-car to stop. I punched the button a couple of times, but nothing happened. I wasn't nervous, but I thought maybe I'd better not wait for the elevator. The clock on the wall said six-twelve, so I decided to walk up. Six flights wouldn't kill me.

It took less than a minute. I still had more than two left.

The stairwell door at the fifteenth floor was locked. I pounded on it, but nothing happened. Now it was six-thirteen, and I started to panic. I banged on that door, yelling, "Let me out! Let me out!" Nobody came.

I ran down to the fourteenth floor and that door was locked. I went to the thirteenth, then the twelfth. The doors were all locked and no one was on the other side of any of them.

Every second seemed like a minute, and I could see the clock taking my job down the drain. Here I was right in the C.B.S. building, missing a nationwide show because nobody could hear me screeching in the stairwell beside the elevators.

And what in the world was I doing in the stairwell anyhow?

It was six-fourteen when I got back to the ninth floor, where I could go out the same door I had gone in. There I ran into one of the staff men, who said, "Curt, for the love of Mike, where have you been?"

"Tell you later," I panted as the elevator arrived.

I raced out of it on the fifteenth floor, hustled into the studio and slid into my seat just as the announcer was saying, "And now with the Saturday Night Football Scoreboard—here's Curt Gowdy."

I could hardly breathe, let alone talk. "Ladies and gentlemen," I gasped, "a funny thing happened to me. I got caught in a stairwell—" I fought for air, then managed to add, "I'm going to sit here a minute while somebody else reads the scores."

I shoved the copy at the announcer and leaned back, battling for my breath while hoping I wouldn't catch it because the one thing I wanted to be at that moment was dead.

It took me a minute or so to pick up the broadcast, then I puffed my way through the first half of it. I finally managed to get up steam, but at any moment I expected the sound of organ music that every announcer dreaded in those days. When something went wrong with a show, the music would come on while somebody in another studio would explain that because of circumstances beyond control the program had been interrupted. It was a sure ticket to oblivion for the guy responsible.

Although there wasn't any organ music, I finished the broadcast with my heart in my shoes. I walked out of the studio and took the elevator back to the ninth floor, wondering which C.B.S. vice president—if not the president himself—would be the one to swing the ax on me.

"John, I blew it," I said to Derr. "The elevator didn't come, so I walked up. The stairwell door was locked, and so were all the other doors."

"I heard the show," John said. "You made a nice recovery."

"Am I through?"

"Of course not. Only maybe you learned a little lesson. After this, allow fifteen minutes to get up there, not five. That's cutting it too thin. You never know when an elevator might be delayed or a door locked."

To this day I don't have nightmares like ordinary people. I dream about the time I got caught in a stairwell with a network show seconds away.

When the football season ended I swung right into basketball. With the professional leagues still struggling for survival, college basketball was at its peak. Everyone wanted to play in Madison Square Garden, which drew capacity crowds for big doubleheaders arranged by Ned Irish, the Garden basketball promoter. The New York newspapers went overboard on the sport, and so did the gamblers. One of the most popular features on the sports pages was the chart of basketball odds and point spreads, and millions of dollars changed hands after every game.

This caused a dangerously unhealthy situation, for the pressure on the college boys was terrific. A few close observers saw disaster ahead, but most—including me—were so wrapped up in the excitement of the moment that they discounted the possibility of anything going wrong. It didn't seem conceivable that the gamblers would get to the kids, or that the kids would fall for the gamblers. Yet, with all that money riding on every game, we should have known better.

The appeal to the players was simple. They didn't necessarily have to lose to keep the gamblers happy. Often, all they had to do was win by a margin less than the point spread. If, for example, a team was favored to win by six points, gamblers betting on the underdogs paid some of the boys on the favored team to see that they won by five or less. This was known as shaving points. However, if the margin was only a point or two, the gamblers paid the favored boys to lose. This was called dumping.

The fixers could afford to pay well, for they stood to win tens, even hundreds, of thousands of dollars. But they bought kids for peanuts—five hundred, a thousand, maybe fifteen hundred—while wrecking reputations and careers. It was a vicious racket, spawned by too much pressure and too little supervision.

I didn't know anything about shaving points or dumping games. Basketball was my sport, and I loved it too dearly to believe it could ever be touched by scandal. I broadcast dozens of college games from Madison Square Garden that winter of 1949–50. Some of them were fixed, but I didn't know it. They all looked on the level to me.

That was the first year the Garden used television, although not on a regular basis. Ned Irish tried it for three or four games, with C.B.S. carrying them on a local program. It was my first experience with television, and I enjoyed it. I was fortunate in learning an important lesson early. With the camera on the action, the announcer should have much less to say. You don't have to describe what people can see for themselves. All you have to do is comment on it.

While I was down South with the Yankees for spring training in 1950, Irish phoned to ask me to return to New York to televise the finals of both the N.C.A.A. championships and the National Invitation, the two biggest college basketball tournaments. At that time, both were held in Madison Square Garden. This first national television of basketball was sponsored by Gillette over the American Broadcasting Company network. That didn't mean coast-to-coast, for television then didn't go west of the Rockies.

I got permission from the Yankees to fly to New York from St. Petersburg two weekends in a row. Claire Bee, the Long Island University coach, worked with me, and we broadcast two of the most exciting college games I ever saw. That was the year of the double slam by City College of New York. Nat Holman's great club beat Bradley in both finals, each time by just a few points.

It was the only double slam in the game's history. I doubt if there'll ever be another, because the N.C.A.A. and the National Invitation tournaments are now held in widely scattered locations with no team playing in both.

The betting scandals broke the following winter. By then I had heard rumors, but refused to believe them. I remember one night having dinner with Sparky Stallcup, the Missouri basketball coach, who came into New York for a game with C.C.N.Y. at the Garden. C.C.N.Y. was heavily favored, but Sparky thought his club could win.

"Let me show you the defense I've rigged up," he said. "We can stop these guys."

Sure enough, that night Missouri pulled an upset victory. The C.C.N.Y. boys couldn't do anything right. After the game Stallcup said, "See, Curt? I told you we had a good defensive setup. What did you think of it?"

"It was great," I said.

Not long after that the City College players admitted they threw the Missouri game, among others. Sick as I was about it, I couldn't resist the temptation to send a note to Sparky. It read: "That sure was a great defense you had."

The C.C.N.Y. disclosures triggered the sorriest mess the sports world had known since the Black Sox scandal of 1919. The New York district attorney's office broke the story piecemeal, releasing something new almost every day. Nobody knew where the next blow would fall or whom it would involve.

One night Claire Bee and I were talking about the scandals in Gene Leone's restaurant. Bee took out his billfold, put it on the table, and said, "Curt, I'd stake every dime I own on the integrity of my boys. I'd put my heart on the table, too, and I'd swear my life that none of my kids ever dumped a game or shaved a point."

He'd have lost his money and his heart and his life, for less than a week later it was announced that several members of his Long Island University team had been reached by the fixers.

That winter of 1950–51 Don Dunphy and I did a weekly television show called DuMont Saturday Night at the Garden. We broadcast all the Saturday events from early December to late February over about fifty stations east of the Rocky Mountains. Most of them were basketball doubleheaders, but there were also a few track meets, a horse show, a rodeo, and one or two other spectacles.

We had no control of the commercials, which were handled by the director. He'd say, "Give a cue for the commercial," and after Don or I had done that, they'd switch to the studio to roll a film. They'd cue us when it ended and we'd go on from there.

One night Bob Richards, the great pole vaulter who is

now a successful commercial announcer himself, was trying to become the first man to clear fifteen feet indoors. He had already won the event, and there was a lull while the bar was moved up. As Richards began warming up for a vault, we got the commercial cue, and the studio took over. Just as the film began Richards started pounding down the runway.

"My Lord, Don," I said, "what if he makes it?"

Without taking his eyes off Richards, Dunphy just shook his head. The two of us sat up in the television booth, helplessly watching track history being made and unable to say anything about it. Richards reached the barrier, jammed his pole down in front of it, and, to Don's horror and mine, heaved himself over the bar. His body grazed it on the way down, but it stayed put and he landed in a cloud of sawdust while the whole Garden went mad.

And there we were, watching the last of a filmed commercial on the monitor.

"I knew something like this would happen," Dunphy muttered. "Why didn't they wait a few seconds?"

When we got back on the air, all we could say was, "Bob Richards just became the first pole vaulter to do fifteen feet indoors. We're sorry, but we missed it."

As the 1951 baseball season approached, I looked forward to a new experience. Instead of being the second man to Mel Allen with the Yankees in New York, I was about to become the number one man with the Red Sox in Boston.

The Braves were still there, and up to that time both teams used Jim Britt, who did only home games. Nobody went on the road with either club. The teams shared the same station, the same sponsors, and the same talent. But after the 1950 season the clubs decided to split up. When I went to Boston with the Yankees for the last series with the Red Sox, I heard that Britt wanted to stay with the Braves. That meant the Red Sox job was open.

Although I had traveled with the Yankees for two years I had never met Joe Cronin, then the Red Sox general manager. On our last day in town I went over to him, held out my hand, and said, "Mr. Cronin, I'm Curt Gowdy."

"I know your voice well," he said. "I have a summer place on Cape Cod and we often get New York clearer than Boston. I listen to you whenever our club is at the Stadium."

"Well, Mr. Cronin—" I began.

"Call me Joe."

"I just wanted to ask you something. Is it true you and the Braves will split your broadcasts after this year?"

"That's right, Curt."

"And you'll be looking for a man?"

"We will."

"May I write you a letter?"

"You certainly may," Cronin said.

Back in New York I talked it over with Jerre, not only because any move I made affected her but also because she knew radio. She had majored in it at college and worked in it before we were married. Although she loved New York, she agreed that the top baseball job in Boston was preferable to the second job anywhere.

Before I had a chance to write Cronin he phoned, inviting me to Boston to talk with him and the sponsors of Red Sox broadcasts. During our meeting they discussed my Wyoming accent, and, to my relief, agreed that it would be acceptable.

Then somebody, after asking if I were a Catholic, said, "Not being one might hurt you in this town."

Cronin, a devout Catholic himself, turned and snapped, "You're out of line. We're looking for a baseball broadcaster. We don't care what his religion is."

The subject didn't come up again, but it bothered me. After everyone had left, and I was ready to head for the airport, I said, "Joe, if I come up here I want to be judged on my merits as an announcer. If people are going to worry about my religion, this job isn't for me."

"Nobody's going to worry about your religion," Cronin said. "You just come here and do a good job covering Red Sox games. That's the only thing that will count."

We shook hands, and I returned to New York completely satisfied. The Red Sox were a wonderful organization. Their owner, Tom Yawkey, was a sportsman and a gentleman for whom everyone had the highest regard. From my own experience, I recognized Cronin as the kind of man I wanted to work for. The job itself represented the realization of all my ambitions. At the time there were only sixteen major league teams. To be the top announcer for one of them was the answer to a sports broadcaster's prayer.

Back in New York Dan Topping, co-owner with Del Webb of the Yankees, was encouraging but with reservations.

"Are you sure you're doing the right thing?" he said. "This is New York, not Podunk. You're doing very well here. Your Garden broadcasts are giving you a big name all over the country. You've got a great future. This is the center of everything in your business."

"That's right," I agreed. "But the biggest job is baseball, and I'll be the second man here behind Mel for a long, long time. I think I'm better off being the first man somewhere else, especially Boston."

"I suppose you're right," Topping said. "But I don't think you should go there as an employee of the sponsors or the radio station. Both could change, and then you'd be out. You must work for the ball club. Let me talk it over with Joe Cronin."

He picked up the phone and called Cronin on the spot. I heard only Topping's end of the conversation, but there were obviously no problems. A week or so later I signed a contract with the Red Sox. I've been working for them ever since.

8

At nine o'clock on the morning after my appointment as the Red Sox broadcaster was announced, the phone rang at my apartment on West 54th Street.

"Mr. Gowdy?"

"Yes."

"You don't know me. My name is Joe Costanza. I'm from Boston. I read that you're going to be the Red Sox announcer and I'd like to apply for the job of statistician for your broadcasts—"

He talked for several minutes, telling me how well he knew the Red Sox, how anxious he was to get into baseball, and how much he'd enjoy working with me. I finally interrupted him with, "Well, that's fine. We'll probably need a statistician and I'll be glad to consider you. Why don't you write me a letter?"

"I'd rather talk to you personally," he said.

"I don't know when I'll be in Boston."

"You don't have to go there to see me. I'm right down here in the lobby of your apartment."

"You are?" I said. "How did you get here?"

"I found out from the Red Sox where you lived, and rode all night on a bus from Boston."

"Have you had breakfast?"

"No."

"Come on up," I said. "Anyone who'll ride a bus all night just to see me has a breakfast coming to him."

Jerre and I liked Joe on sight. An absolute nut on baseball, he sat and talked about it all morning. We had a sportscasters' lunch at Al Schacht's restaurant that day, so

I took him with me. I introduced him to Mel Allen, Bill Stern, Ted Husing, and Red Barber, and he was in seventh heaven. Before he got a bus back to Boston I promised to hire him if the sponsors had no objections. They didn't, and Joe came to work for me. Getting him was one of the smartest moves I ever made.

Joe was the Red Sox fan to end all Red Sox fans. He knew all about everyone on the 1951 team and all the teams before it. He had read every scrap of information he could find about Red Sox ballplayers. He knew where they came from, what they had done, and what could be expected of them. Even though his knowledge was only that of a fan, it was the most extensive of any fan's I ever knew.

Perhaps even more important for my purposes, Joe knew Boston and New England. This is a proud, provincial area, jammed with sizable cities and towns and historical landmarks, many of which are not pronounced the way they're spelled. In Cheyenne, Wyoming, I could be forgiven for calling Worcester "Wor-sester" and Haverhill "Ha-ver-hill" and Gloucester "Glow-sester," but not in Boston, Massachusetts. There were dozens of name traps for me to fall into, and I didn't miss many.

One day Carl Haffenreffer, treasurer of the Narragansett Brewing Company, one of our sponsors, phoned and said, "Curt, we're delighted with your broadcasts and glad to have you with us, but will you do us a favor? Get somebody who's lived in Boston all his life to teach you to talk a little New England English. Guys in bars are complaining to our distributors that you're murdering the names of their home towns."

Joe Costanza got a list of all the communities within range of my voice, which meant everywhere in New England except southern Connecticut. The Red Sox network included over forty radio stations, so every time I butchered the name of a town thousands of listeners squirmed. Joe drilled me and drilled me. It took a couple of years, but I finally learned.

One thing I never learned was the proper Boston accent. When I first went there I got letters from teachers, scientists, college professors, cops, firemen, doctors, merchants, politicians, bankers, Beacon Hill bluebloods, South Boston Irishmen, East Boston Italians, kids, grownups, priests, ministers, rabbis—just about everyone you can imagine—criticizing my accent. For a while I was afraid it was more than staid old New England could take, but I guess the people got used to it. That took a couple of years, too.

Jerre was expecting the first of our three children when it was time for me to go to Sarasota, Florida, for Red Sox spring training in 1951. Cheryl arrived at Doctors Hospital in New York on April 14. We had a Sunday doubleheader with the Athletics in Philadelphia that day. The minute it ended I rushed to the airport and flew to New York, arriving at the hospital half an hour before the baby was born. My mother had come from Cheyenne to be with Jerre, and Trevor Adams, our closest friend in New York, was doing the floor-pacing for me. We later named the younger of our two boys after him. The older is Curt, Jr.

I didn't meet Tom Yawkey until after the season began. He sent for me when he got into town, smiled, shook hands, and said, "I just want to tell you how delighted we are to have you with us. You don't have to worry about anything around here. This is probably the most intelligent baseball town in the country. Boston has had major league ball for seventy-five years, and its fans know the game better than the fans anywhere. You can't kid them. Just give them their baseball straight. Don't try to phony anything up or do a lot of synthetic cheering on the air. They'll do the cheering, and it won't be synthetic. All they want you to do is tell them what's going on.

"Don't let criticism bother you," Yawkey added. "You'll get plenty. You're a westerner with a New York background, fresh from the hated Yankees. That won't sit well at first with a lot of New Englanders, but they'll get over it. And remember—we're behind you a hundred per cent."

If there's a more enthusiastic fan in America than Joe Costanza, it's Tom Yawkey. He loves baseball so much that he can't get enough of it. He hears several games at once on different radios, using short wave when he has to. If there's a big league ball game anywhere, he listens to it. On Red Sox off days, I've seen him with three radios tuned directly to three different cities. Sometimes he's up until two or three in the morning for games on the West Coast.

He lives in South Carolina and has an apartment in New York, but is in Boston most of the summer, usually starting about the middle of May. There, he spends almost all his time at the ball park. He gets there early in the morning, works there, eats there, and goes back to his hotel at night. He never misses a game when the Red Sox are in town. When they're on the road he listens to the broadcasts or watches when we televise in a lounge off the Fenway Park executive offices.

He's sociable without being social. A friendly, regular guy, he'll talk baseball with anyone who happens to be around, yet he's very shy. He dislikes the spotlight, hates formal functions, doesn't care to be seen in public, and rarely submits to interviews. He's a philanthropist in the true sense of the word—a man who gives generously but prefers to remain anonymous. He's a marvelous boss, the most thoughtful and loyal man I have ever known. His employees, all the way down to the clubhouse boys and the ground help, absolutely worship him. He's so sensitive to other people's feelings that he finds it an ordeal to fire anyone, although he has had to do it occasionally.

When he first bought the Red Sox in 1933 he was very close to his ballplayers, but in those days they were his contemporaries. Not many players know him personally today, even his own. Many have had letters from him, however.

When someone does something he admires, or is recovering from a serious illness or injury, or needs a morale lift, Yawkey writes him.

He knows of my passion for fishing, and whenever he finds new lures or flies he's enjoyed using he sends a few to me, along with a note saying something like, "Try these. I think they're great." He's an avid newspaper reader who sends pertinent clippings to his friends along with a line or two of comment. I've had dozens from him.

After I got home from a South American fishing trip, he heard I had neglected to take a landing net. One day I received a wire reading: "Seventy-five hundred miles without a landing net. What happened?" It was signed: "T.A.Y." He ribbed me about that for half the next baseball season.

I became friendly with Ted Williams more through fishing than baseball. Williams is a complex character who resembles Yawkey in some ways. He disliked the spotlight fully as much, but, unlike Yawkey, couldn't stay out of it. He is Yawkey's kind of philanthropist, giving generously but anonymously. Not that Williams is a shrinking violet. Although he has violent likes and dislikes, he enjoys meeting people and can talk for hours on many subjects.

When he played for the Red Sox his favorites were hitting and fishing, but he was almost equally well informed about business, the stock market, photography, nature, and heaven knows what else. He was hardest to talk to during the baseball season, easiest when fishing during the off season. Although I traveled with him for years I rarely saw him on the road. But I spent many wonderful hours fishing with him off the Florida Keys near his home in Islamorada, where we talked baseball until it was coming out of our ears.

No man lived who knew more about hitting. Williams loved to meet a challenge, to face a promising new young pitcher, to solve whatever problem was presented. I think that was what made him great. He could hit any pitcher after watching him a few times, and the hotter the pitcher the better he liked it. His awareness of the law of averages kept him from having any illusions. He knew the odds were always against the batter, but that only made him work harder for perfection. Pitchers realized this, and quaked in their shoes when he came to the plate. I never met one who faced Williams with real confidence. All were happy to see him out of there.

When Williams got back from Korea after serving his second hitch as a Marine pilot, he couldn't wait to face Herb Score, Cleveland's young left-handed fireball artist. Score, who had a fantastic rookie season, looked like the second coming of Lefty Grove. He might have topped Grove's records if he hadn't nearly lost an eye when hit by a line drive a third of the way through his third season in the majors.

We got into Cleveland before that mishap, and Score faced us the first day. Before the game Williams asked for the hundredth time, "Is he as good as they say he is?" And for the hundredth time, everyone he asked replied, "Better."

By this time Williams had worked himself up like a fighter about to go into the ring. He had read everything about Score he could find, and talked to people all over the league about him. He didn't take his eyes off the kid warming up before the game. He was so anxious to bat against Score that he paced the dugout until it was time for him to go to the on-deck circle.

I don't recall how the count ran when Williams finally got to the plate, but I do remember that Score almost beaned him with a fast ball. As always when a pitch came close, Williams barely flicked his head, and the ball whizzed by within a fraction of an inch of it. Ted belted the next pitch to left-center—the opposite field for him—for a double. Before the game ended he smashed another Score fast ball over the left-field fence. He faced the youngster once more before Score's accident, got a couple more hits, and ended up batting .500 against him.

Williams loved fast-ball pitchers. The more they had on the ball the better he liked it, because that presented a challenge to him. On the other hand, he couldn't stand "junk" pitchers like Eddie Lopat or Stubby Overmire. Their slow stuff drove him crazy, and he never hit it well.

He rose to occasions, and, in fact, was at his best just before going somewhere or just after coming back. On his last time at bat before leaving for Korea in April of 1952, he smashed a home run off Dizzy Trout of the Tigers. Williams rounded the bases, went into the dugout, down the runway to the clubhouse, took off his Red Sox uniform, showered, got into his civilian clothes, and was just leaving to report to the Marines for duty when the game ended.

Over a year later, in August of 1953, he appeared as a pinch-hitter the day after he got out of the service, and belted a tremendous homer into the right-field bleachers off Mike Garcia of the Indians.

The following March Williams broke his shoulder in the first ten minutes of spring training, and a six-inch steel pin was inserted to keep it together. He rejoined the Red Sox in Baltimore on May 16, and flied out as a pinch-hitter. The next day he told Manager Lou Boudreau he could play, so Boudreau started him in left field in a doubleheader at Detroit.

In the clubhouse before the game I asked Williams how he felt.

"Not good," he said. "Every time I swing my shoulder kills me. I can't take a full cut, and the ball doesn't look big to me. If I find I'm doing the club more harm than good I'll have to get out of there."

He didn't harm anybody but Detroit pitchers that day. In the two games he got nine hits, including two home runs, in ten times at bat. When Casey Stengel, then the Yankees' manager, read about it the next morning, he said,

"I think I'll get some of them steel pins to put in my guys' shoulders."

I'll never forget Ted Williams' last game, on September 26, 1960, at Fenway Park. It was a gray, overcast day in Boston. I was master-of-ceremonies in a brief farewell to Williams at home plate before the game. The Boston Chamber of Commerce had a gift for him, and Mayor John F. Collins a personal presentation on behalf of the city.

I spent the morning at the studio cutting some commercials, and arrived at the ball park a few minutes before the ceremony. I had no notes, no speech, not even much in the way of organized thoughts for my introduction. Yet, because I felt deeply that we were about to witness the end of a baseball era, I think I gave one of the best talks of my career in presenting Williams for the last time.

It was the last home game for the Red Sox, who would close the season in New York. Although nothing was at stake, over ten thousand fans braved the elements to come out and see Williams bow out of a picture he had dominated for more than twenty years.

I looked up at the crowd and said, "As we all know, this is the final home game for the greatest hitter who ever lived—Ted Williams." Then I touched on Williams' arrival in Boston as a skinny kid in 1939, and spoke, not of his many records but of his dramatic style. I mentioned his controversial personality and the thrills he had given us all.

In closing, I spoke of his intense pride, for that was his outstanding characteristic. Williams couldn't stand the thought of looking bad. That was why he had spent so many hours in study and extra practice, and I wanted to put that idea over before the crowd.

"Pride is what made Williams great," I said. "He's a champion and a thoroughbred."

When Williams stepped up to the microphone to say goodbye, those ten thousand fans sounded like one hundred thousand.

As always, he rose to the occasion, and, as always, he waited until the psychological moment. On his first time up against southpaw Steve Barber, he drew a pass. He led off the third inning against Jack Fisher, who was born in 1939, the year Williams broke into the majors. That time Ted drove a 1-1 pitch deep to right-center, where Jackie Brandt made the catch.

In the fifth Williams yanked us all out of our seats when he smashed a tremendous drive to deep right-center, but Al Pilarcik, the Orioles' right fielder, raced to the bullpen area at the 380-foot mark and pulled it down leaning against the fence. Everyone sat back in disappointment.

Williams came up for the last time with one out in the eighth inning. The crowd rose and gave him a standing ovation which lasted two full minutes while Fisher stood quietly on the mound. Then everything went silent.

Williams stepped into the batter's box and the young Baltimore right-hander threw his first pitch. It was low for a ball. The next was a fast ball, a little high and out of the strike zone, the kind Williams rarely swung at. Perhaps because he wasn't sure he would see anything better, he took a mighty cut at it, but missed. That made the count one and one.

Fisher leaned forward for the sign while Williams, just as he always had, stood stock still at the plate. It was so quiet my own voice sounded unusually loud as I talked into the mike.

The pitch, another fast ball, came in waist high toward the outside of the plate. Williams snapped his bat around, and as ball and bat met, there was a roar, "There it goes!"

And there it went, over the bullpen barrier, over the bullpen itself, and well into the right-field bleachers. As Williams circled the bases, head down as he habitually did on hitting a home run, people yelled and screamed and whistled and applauded. His head was still down as he crossed the plate, and he ran into the dugout without tipping his cap, for this was his trade mark.

The ovation lasted five minutes. The people wanted a last look at him. I heard later that some of his teammates urged him at least to poke his head out, but that wouldn't have been in character. Williams remained out of sight.

It was a marvelous climax to a fantastic career. Nobody was surprised when Williams announced his retirement after the game. The Red Sox finished the season on the road without him. Not one person—Yawkey, the fans, the other Red Sox players, Williams himself, even the writers—wanted anything to spoil the perfection of his exit.

Williams' dislike for the Boston writers dated back long before my time. He never talked much to me about it beyond making a contemptuous reference here and there. His favorite sportswriters were Arthur Daley of the New York *Times,* Frank Graham of the New York *Journal-American,* and Arthur Sampson of the Boston *Herald.* He thought most of the others, especially in Boston and Cleveland, were "bush," which to Williams was the supreme insult. Yet he always went out of his way to help writers from smaller cities and towns, many of whom swear by him to this day. Only the writers from the big metropolitan papers bothered him.

On the other hand, he was wonderful with radio and television people. For years I've had a program called "Dugout Interviews" before Red Sox games, and Williams often appeared on it. He had a good voice, projected his personality well, and wasn't afraid to express an opinion. He always insisted on knowing ahead of time what we were going to talk about, then spoke fluently and well. He was just as cooperative with other announcers, both in Boston and elsewhere, in large cities and small.

I still see Williams occasionally. His job with Sears keeps him busy only at certain times of the year, so now he can fish to his heart's content. I asked him not long ago if he misses the excitement of baseball.

"I'm happy," he replied. "I love my freedom. I go where I please, do as I please, live the way I please. And now I'm able to go fishing in summer as well as winter."

"Do you follow baseball?"

"I sure do," he said. "I love the game as much as ever. But I love it as a fan, not as a player. And I don't miss it a bit."

Williams' only connection with baseball today is as a Red Sox batting coach in spring training. It is, I'm sure, the only connection he wants.

9

My back trouble was always with me, but I learned to live with it. The pain was intense when I got tired or remained in one position too long. Traveling could be an ordeal, and I was never able to drive a car for more than a few hours at a time. I rested a good deal, sometimes wore a brace, and had periodic checkups at the Leahy Clinic in Boston. The condition was chronic but not intolerable, and as long as I was careful it didn't figure to get any worse.

Much as I loved sports, my only outdoor recreation was fishing, and I had to pussyfoot my way through that. A boulder, an unexpected obstacle, a sudden twist on a line could throw me out of whack for a week. I seemed to be in more danger playing than working. My job never resulted in any more than the normal amount of discomfort.

I kept pretty busy. Besides the Red Sox games, I had a radio show six evenings a week all the year around on Boston's station WHDH. For some years, I worked in the off-season for the National Broadcasting Company, doing college football in the autumn and pro basketball in the winter. Baseball announcers everywhere are in demand for speaking engagements, and I had my share. I didn't take a regular vacation, but didn't feel I needed one. I enjoyed my work and had plenty of time off after baseball ended. If I wanted to get away for a few days, I taped my radio shows in advance, or arranged for someone else to do them. And the trips to Sarasota when the Red Sox trained there were really more recreation than work.

In 1957, not long after our youngest child, Trevor, was born, I took the family there for spring training. About a month after we arrived, a drunken driver, infuriated because he thought I had cut him out while driving with Jerre to a Red Sox press party, rammed the back of my car with his. He then got out of his car to throw a punch at me while I was sitting at the wheel of mine. I ducked away and his fist grazed my jaw. I would have been better off if I had let him hit me.

In dodging him I twisted my back. I felt a pain shoot all the way down my legs, sharp and searing, as though someone had shoved a hot poker along my spine. We went to the party, but stayed only a short time. Back home, I took a sedative before retiring and slept pretty well, then woke up the next morning in agony.

That was the beginning of the longest, most painful, most frightening siege of illness I have ever known. Except for a few token appearances at the ball park I missed the entire 1957 season, and not for a year after that could I function normally. If it hadn't been for Jerre, who gave up everything else to nurse, encourage, and badger me back to health, I never would have made it.

While I was sick I had no appreciation of the burden she carried. I was so preoccupied with my own troubles that I accepted hers as a matter of course. Only after my recovery did I begin to understand what she had been through. Everywhere I went I met people who knew better than I what a remarkable job she had done. She gave up everything to take care of me, and she handled me perfectly through all the various stages of my illness.

Doctors who treated me were so impressed with Jerre that they even told some of their other patients about her. To this day, I see people whose first words are, "That wife of yours must be a marvel. Dr. Poppen [or Dr. Parker, or whoever else it might be] thinks the world of her."

Jack Fadden, the Red Sox trainer, was the first to examine me. He realized my trouble was beyond his skills, and sent me back to Boston for checkups by Leahy Clinic doctors at the New England Baptist Hospital. The flight home was murder, and when I arrived it was all I could do to hobble to a taxi.

At the hospital they pushed and pulled and stretched and X-rayed and tested me. My back got worse and worse, and pretty soon I was practically climbing the walls. The tests were still going on when Jerre arrived. By then I was groggy from medication, half out of my mind from pain, frightened that I'd end up a hopeless cripple, and worried to death about my job. As I lay helplessly on an orthopedic mattress in the hospital, the days were rolling relentlessly by toward the beginning of the baseball season.

Jerre spent much of her time at the hospital with me, leaving the children in the care of Mrs. Lilla Curley, a practical nurse who had come to help out when Trevvy was born and had accompanied us to Sarasota. The older children knew and loved her, since she had been with us before, so Jerre had no qualms about asking her to take charge of the household until we could make other arrangements.

The baseball season began with me still in the hospital. Tom Yawkey came into town early that year to receive the Great Heart Award from the Boston chapter of the Variety Club for his contributions to children's cancer research, through the Jimmy Fund. The Red Sox have raised millions of dollars for the Jimmy Fund, which they still support, and it has been my own favorite charity ever since I came to the ball club. I was supposed to emcee the Variety Club dinner in Yawkey's honor, but Bob Murphy, my broadcasting partner, had to fill in for me.

Yawkey came to see me at the hospital. "Curt," he said, "don't worry about a thing. You'll always have a job with the Red Sox, no matter how sick you are or how long it lasts. The only thing that counts is your health."

Dr. James Poppen, world-famous chief neurosurgeon of the Leahy Clinic, who had taken charge of my case, was opposed to another operation and convinced that only time and rest would straighten me out. Torn adhesions, inflamed spinal nerve roots, and severe muscle spasms were causing the pain, from which there was no immediate hope of release, but he told me it would eventually subside. Although he thought I should stay in the hospital I insisted on going home. The tests were all over, and I wanted to be with my family.

Jerre took me home the Saturday of Easter weekend, and I went right to bed. We lived in Wellesley Hills, not far from Dr. A. S. (Ace) Parker, one of the doctors who had been taking care of me, and he dropped in to see how I was doing. One look at me writhing in pain was all he needed. He gave me a shot of Demerol and said he'd stick around. He ended up spending the night, giving me shots as long as he dared, but they had no more effect than sugar pills.

Dr. Bob Wise, a neighbor and good friend of ours, who was an X-ray man at the Leahy Clinic, came over that morning. He and Ace went into a huddle, then Dr. Parker came in and said, "Curt, we're going to take you back to the hospital as soon as they have a room available. You can't go on like this. I gave you enough dope last night to put you in twilight sleep, and you're still in pain."

While we were waiting to hear from the hospital, Mel Allen, in town with the Yankees, called to ask if he could see me. Jerre told him to hurry on out, and he was there within half an hour. He stopped in my room, but when he saw the shape I was in, remained only a few minutes. I remember his visit as in a dream.

Out in the front yard, he gave Jerre some of the best advice she ever had. "You can't carry this burden alone," he told her. "You've got to have somebody to lean on, somebody you can talk to and confide in. Don't you have a close relative who can stay with you until Curt recovers from this thing?"

Jerre had just lost her father, and her mother was alone in Oklahoma. At Mel's insistence, Jerre phoned her. Her arrival was good for everybody, including herself. Our plight gave her something other than her own grief to think about. She spent many hours with me and many more with the children, and relieved Jerre in countless other ways. I don't know what we would have done without her.

At the hospital they put me in a body cast, which gave me some semblance of relief although I couldn't move. Three weeks after getting home I woke up one morning feeling as if someone had poured gasoline down my legs and then set fire to it. Jerre put in a hurry call for Ace Parker, who immediately saw what was wrong. I had literally eaten my way into traction.

During those early weeks of awful pain I had lost a lot of weight because I couldn't take much nourishment. I was at my thinnest when the body cast went on. With the pain less intense I started eating again. As I gained weight the body cast rode up like a corset, stretching my spine and the inflamed spinal nerve roots with it. A couple of technicians from the hospital came out to cut the thing off. That relieved the immediate pressure, but left me with the pains and spasms I had before.

Instead of getting another body cast, I went to see Dr. Otto Aufranc of the Massachusetts General Hospital, the orthopedic surgeon who once operated on Arthur Godfrey's hip. He built me a plaster shell which I could get into and out of at will. It was so comfortable that for a while I practically lived in it, and it took months to wean me away from it.

I didn't leave my room for weeks. As the pain receded a little I got so restless that Jerre said one day, "Why don't you try to do your evening show from here? Maybe the station will send out an engineer to get you set up and somebody in the studio can write your copy."

Bill McGrath, the WHDH manager, was delighted with the idea. He sent two engineers out to the house, and they hooked up all the necessary equipment. Joe Costanza, who stopped by almost every day either before or after ball games when he was in town, insisted on writing the first script and bringing it out himself.

As the time approached for me to go on the air, I felt like the rookie I was when I did that six-man football game in Cheyenne fifteen years before. Much of the pain in my back was temporarily replaced by butterflies in my stomach. I started clearing my throat, and I must have looked scared because Joe said, "Don't panic, pal. You've done this a million times before."

The next thing I knew, the engineer was pointing at me. I said, "This is Curt Gowdy," and started reading the script. To me, my voice sounded far away, but scores of people wrote and called to tell me it sounded great. It didn't, of course, but nobody said so at the time. Only later did they admit I sounded weak and reedy and not at all like myself.

The engineers left the equipment in my room, and came out every day after that. Sometimes I was in such pain I couldn't broadcast, but most of the time I managed. Jerre and the doctors—especially Ace Parker and Bob Wise, who dropped by nearly every day—encouraged me to keep it up even when I was in pain. They all knew I had a long way to go, and that the broadcasts were helping my morale.

Although still heavily dependent on the plaster shell Dr. Aufranc had made, I began moving around the house a little in early June.

One day that month Jerre decided to take me to the ball park.

"I think you ought to do an inning or two," she said.

I thought of the ride to Fenway Park, the trip up to the roof, and the narrow ship's ladder leading from there into the broadcasting booth, and shuddered.

"I'll never make it," I said.

"Well, you should try. I'm going to call Joe Cronin and see what he thinks."

Cronin thought it was a great idea. "Curt won't have to go down that ship's ladder," he told Jerre. "We'll set him up in one of the booths next to the press box upstairs."

We picked a beautiful sunny day for the experiment. After phoning the ball park to let them know I was coming, Jerre helped me into my clothes, then she and her mother put me into the back of the station wagon. While I lay there, sweating and shaking, Jerre got behind the wheel and started driving about ten miles an hour.

The trip was a nightmare. The slightest bump went through me like a hot needle. Every two minutes I yelled, "Aren't we there yet?" and Jerre answered, "Not quite." It took an hour for the normal twenty-five-minute ride, and I was exhausted when we arrived.

Jerre backed the car up to the pass gate, where Joe Costanza and the late Johnny Pohlmeyer, Yawkey's personal aide, were waiting for me with a wheelchair. It took them ten minutes just to get me out of the wagon and five more to settle me in the chair. Then, as I constantly repeated, "Take it easy," they pushed me up the ramp to the back of the grandstand and into the Red Sox offices, at the end of which was a private flight of stairs to the roof.

Getting up those was a real operation. Someone went ahead with the wheelchair while Joe and Johnny gently worked me along like a crate of eggs. They did a tremendous job, but the pain was so terrible that when I finally got to the top I wanted to stay there forever. I didn't see how they could get me down again.

They installed me in a booth beside the press box and I actually announced half an inning. I hardly knew what was happening on the field and my listeners must have known even less. I couldn't concentrate on the game, let alone tell anyone about it. I've done some pretty bad broadcasts in my time, but that was the worst. I went home determined not to go back until I could do at least a passable job. Except for one midsummer visit for a Jimmy Fund exhibition game between the Red Sox and the Braves, I confined all my subsequent Fenway Park trips to the last month of the season.

However, I continued to do my evening radio show from my room at home. Although never free from pain, I could relax in my shell. I often lay in it throughout the broadcast. One day someone at station WBZ, which televised Red Sox games over Channel 4 at the time, suggested I do an out-of-town broadcast from my home. Since I wouldn't appear on the screen and could use the shell if I needed it, I agreed.

The engineers installed a direct line into my bedroom from Municipal Stadium in Cleveland, where the game was played. I watched a monitor at the foot of my bed, and had Bob Murphy, who was in Cleveland, on the telephone as I talked into the microphone. Whenever a ball went out of range of the camera, Murphy would say, "fly to right," or "grounder to short," or whatever it happened to be, and I'd broadcast it that way.

Although Murphy was keeping me posted on what happened, New England fans heard only my voice, so it sounded as if I were right on the scene. They knew I wasn't, of course, since the arrangement was all explained beforehand. I did four innings without too much strain. Unique as it was, my bedroom telecast attracted national attention in broadcasting publications.

I had to be doped up to make the Jimmy Fund exhibition. It was even worse than the first visit to Fenway Park because the game was at night. Despite the pain and the fact that I sounded like death warmed over during my one inning on the air, I had no regrets. The cause was worth the effort.

My progress was so slow that there was no appreciable change until September. By then I didn't seem quite so slavishly dependent on the shell, although heaven knows I used it often enough. One day I suggested to Jerre that we try going to the ball park again. The trip was still a pretty big deal, but not half as bad as it had been before. I still lay down in the back of the station wagon and Jerre still had to drive very carefully and slowly. Getting in and out of the car wasn't so hard and, once at Fenway Park, the boys didn't have to lift me bodily up and down the stairs. I went to half a dozen games and did two or three innings each time. I wouldn't have won any amateur hour prizes, but I felt a little more comfortable at the microphone and gave my listeners a reasonable idea of what was happening on the field.

As I got away from the shell, which had become sort of a pacifier, I moved around more. I got dressed every day, walked around outside a little, and found that I could be fairly comfortable in a back brace. I continued to do my evening broadcasts from home, but one day in October I asked Jerre to drive me to the studio.

Station WHDH was then in the Paine Furniture building, about a mile farther from Wellesley than Fenway Park. When I was settled in the back of the wagon, Jerre started out. I let her drive faster this time, squawking only occasionally instead of constantly, as I had before.

Joe Costanza was waiting in front of the door. He escorted us up the elevator. The operator, the reception girl, the other announcers, the engineers, and Bill McGrath, the station manager, all greeted me like the long-lost colleague I was, and I felt quite at home. I didn't go in every day at first, but I was able to later in the month, and by November I let them remove the equipment from my house.

After a while, I could sit up front with Jerre when she drove me in. Later, with the help of an orthopedic seat which I still use, I did the driving myself. Jerre always went with me, for I was still in pain, and never knew when I would need help. She continued to drop everything to be with me. I knew this couldn't go on forever, but I wasn't yet ready to do anything on my own.

When it was time to go to Sarasota for 1958 spring training, Jerre decided to leave the children home with her mother so she could concentrate on taking care of me. We had just moved into a new house and there would have been plenty for Jerre to do at home, but she felt getting me resettled in my job was more important. She was right, of course. I couldn't possibly have got through spring training without her. There were too many days when I couldn't move from my room, too many nights when I still woke up in a cold sweat from the pain.

She bridged the gap between home and the baseball season for which spring training was a dry run. Sometimes I got to the ball park, sometimes I didn't. When I didn't, Bob Murphy handled everything himself, for we were the only announcers there. Since I couldn't take any of the trips, which were mostly by bus around Florida, he had to do all those games, too, but he never complained or showed the slightest annoyance.

The season opened in Washington, and I knew this was the time for me to go out on my own. Jerre had carried me this far; I had to do the rest myself. She was willing to go to Washington with me, but I wouldn't let her.

I didn't sleep a wink the night before the team left Boston. I had a lot of muscle spasm and was in almost constant pain. Jerre phoned Ace Parker, and he came over in the morning to give me a shot.

"Don't go with the team," he said. "Get all the rest you can and if you feel any better you can fly down tomorrow."

I had another bad night, and could hardly move the next morning. I phoned Bob Murphy and told him he and Bill Crowley, who had joined our broadcasting team, would have to do the game without me.

Upset and discouraged, I plaintively asked Jerre if she thought I'd ever be well again.

"Of course you'll be well," she said. "You're improving all the time."

"Well, what's the matter with me now?"

"You're nervous and excited. Now calm down and stop worrying. And for heaven's sake, get some rest."

Jerre's nerves must have been worn thin by then, but that wasn't why she spoke sharply. She meant to be just as tough as she sounded, for she knew it was essential that I stop feeling sorry for myself. I resented it then. I didn't know her apparent impatience was deliberate. But this was the only way she could handle me at that point if she were ever to get me to resume my normal activities.

She practically hounded me into taking a nap in my shell, which I still used when the pain got bad. That time I actually did sleep, and was ready to take off for Washington in the afternoon. The shell went with me. I was lying in it on the floor of my hotel room when Murphy and Crowley came to see me after dinner.

"I'm not nuts," I said. "I'm just happier on the floor than the bed."

"Will you feel like working tomorrow?" Bob asked.

"I'll work."

I did, too. And, although I had some setbacks, I worked most games all season. I missed two or three a month during the first part of the year, for that was when I had my worst spells. The toughest ball parks were the ones without elevators—Fenway Park and Municipal Stadium in Cleveland. Stairs and ramps were more than I could handle, so I had to use wheelchairs. I hated them, especially in Boston, where I was known. I always rode with my head down, hoping nobody would recognize me.

I rationed my energy the way a shipwrecked man rations his food. I used it only while actually working. The rest of the time I loafed, at the house or in the yard at home, in my hotel room on the road. I never went anywhere I didn't have to go, never did anything I didn't have to do. I went to bed early and stayed in bed late.

But I improved. The bouts of intense pain became fewer and farther between as the season progressed. By the end of July I could drive alone to the Boston ball park and walk up to the radio booth without help. It took a long time, for I stopped to rest after every few steps, but I made it. Anything was better than that wheelchair.

One September afternoon, while I was sunning myself in the back yard, I had a phone call from Tom Gallery in New York.

"How are you doing, Curt?" he asked.

"Pretty well," I said.

"How would you like to do the World Series?"

I couldn't believe my ears.

"How would I like to do the—what?" I said.

"The World Series. We want you to team up with Mel Allen."

"You're not kidding me, Tom?"

"Of course not. What do you say?"

"I say I should hope to kiss a pig I'd like to do the World Series," I yelled into the phone. "I say I'd do the World Series if they had to take me there in an ambulance. I say thanks a million, and I just hope I can do the job you want."

That call from Tom Gallery was one of the greatest thrills of my life. I had never done a World Series and, since announcers were usually picked from the winning cities and the Red Sox weren't going anywhere, I never expected to. Besides being a real honor, it was a marvelous expression of Tom's faith in me. That alone meant more than anything else.

The Series, between the Braves and the Yankees, opened in Milwaukee. Wearing my steel brace and armed with a prescription in case I needed a pain-killer, I flew there alone, checked in at the Hotel Schroeder, and went right to the ball park to watch the teams work out. That was a mistake. I had taken the flight, including a change in Chicago, very well, but standing around the field stiffened me all up. I took a couple of sleeping pills and spent a miserable night rolling around on the floor of my hotel room.

At breakfast I said to Allen, "Mel, this is terrible. My back is killing me, and I don't think I'm going to make the game this afternoon."

He handled me the way Jerre would have handled me, the only way I could have been handled under the circumstances. He got tough and he stayed tough.

"You'll make the game if I have to carry you myself," he said. "Don't you have anything to kill the pain?"

"A prescription."

"Well, let's get it filled."

Half an hour later I took the first of several pills. My back still bothered me, but Allen ignored my complaints. When it was time to go to County Stadium, he bundled me into a cab and out we went.

"I don't think I can do it," I said, as I hobbled out of the taxi.

"You'll do it," Allen said. "Now come on and stop griping."

He kept after me right up to game time. I was still protesting when the producer pointed at me as the red eye lit up on the camera. I was on N.B.C. television, and I wouldn't be off for four and a half innings.

"Good afternoon, ladies and gentlemen . . ." I began, and then, forgetting my back and everything else but the ball game, I went to work.

It was the best therapy I ever had.

10

Football is a complicated game, but there wasn't anything very complicated about covering it until television came along. When I first began doing college football in Oklahoma, all it took was an engineer and a couple of announcers, one for play-by-play, the other for color. On long trips the color man was sometimes left home to save expenses.

The engineer would set up one mike on the roof, suspend another below the roof for crowd noises, and put one or two in the radio booth. We were supposed to do a certain number of commercials per game, but used our own judgment as to exactly when. There were no producers, directors, technicians, agency men, nor any of the other reinforcements who now work a big college or professional football game on television.

About the only ones who look the same are the spotters. Back in the old days we used two, one from each team, and we still use two. A spotter is somebody thoroughly familiar with one team. We always tried to get some bright senior who never missed a game, perhaps the sports editor of the college paper or somebody like that. His job was to sit beside the play-by-play announcer and be ready to answer instantly any question about who did what on his own team.

Some announcers depended too heavily on spotters for key players, such as ball-carriers and passers—the men everyone in the stands would be watching. I've always felt that the announcer who couldn't see them for himself didn't belong on the job. Football required intensive homework even before television. Every competent announcer spent hours memorizing players' numbers so that he would at least have the backs and the ends down cold by game time. Today the announcer who doesn't instantly recognize ballcarriers, passers, receivers, punters, place-kickers, key blockers, and tacklers is in trouble. He still has spotters, but only for emergencies or for keeping track of the dozens of substitutes who stream into the game under the multiple-platoon system.

Television has eliminated the "downfield lateral," a handy device invented by a famous sports announcer who had a tendency to call the wrong man carrying the ball on long runs.

"Jones has it," he might say. "He breaks off tackle . . . he's out in the secondary . . . he's *away* . . ."

"It's not Jones—it's Smith," a spotter would whisper, or perhaps the announcer would suddenly realize it himself. Then he would shout into the mike, "He laterals the ball downfield to Smith . . . and Smith scores!"

I've never used the downfield lateral myself. I operate on the theory that when you pull a bloop the best thing to do is admit it.

Television requires much more intensive coverage than radio. On a major college or pro game, there are always at least three announcers, and often more. When we had five in the college All-Star telecast of 1964, somebody remarked, "You need a scorecard for the announcers, not just the ballplayers."

I did the play-by-play, with Paul Christman and Johnny Lujack working on color and expert analysis in the booth with me. Both are former All-America stars and keen students of the game, and both have good voices and good vocabularies. We had Bill Fleming on the field to introduce the players, do spot interviews, and handle the color there. Robert Rieger, the famed sports illustrator and artist, who worked before the game and between the halves, completed our team of announcers.

We had a crew of about seventy that day, including a producer, a director, cameramen, engineers, technical advisers, representatives of sponsors and advertising agencies, specialists, assistants, heavy-duty men and other supernumeraries. This wasn't unusual. The game was telecast in color, which requires more personnel than black-and-white productions. Most nationally televised sports events are in color today.

Where we once used one or two cameras, we now sometimes have as many as eight. In A.B.C. football broadcasts we've had cameras in the booths, on the roof, and at various points of the field. We've had them suspended on cranes over end zones and set low in the stands facing benches, and we've had creepy-peepy cameras ranging along the sidelines. The best roving television cameraman I've ever seen was Mike Friedman of A.B.C., who used to practice for hours learning to move around without jiggling his camera. He could get dramatic closeups of players' faces as they came off the field or of coaches as they strode back and forth in front of the bench. By going straight down the sidelines he could keep up with a zigzagging ballcarrier, holding his camera on his shoulder and shooting as he ran. I once saw a blocker bowl him over and knock his camera out of his hands. Mike just got up, scooped up the camera, and ran down the sidelines, getting some marvelous pictures on the way.

College games are harder to prepare for than pro games. The pro teams have set personnel which changes little throughout the season. College teams are always changing. College boys are more prone to injury—they lack the toughness, smartness, and experience of pros—and newcomers are more likely to come out of nowhere into the spotlight. A sophomore who doesn't even make the fourth team in a preseason depth chart can develop overnight into a college regular. Also, you rarely see the same college team twice in one season, but you are likely to see the same pro club four or five times.

While the college games require more preparation, the most fun I ever had was televising the N.C.A.A. college football series on A.B.C. in 1961 and 1962. The crew was young, the series new, the venture a success, and everyone had a wonderful time.

Up to that time, N.B.C. seemed to have a stranglehold on college football telecasts, partly because nobody else made serious bids for them. A.B.C. had had college football, but gave it up because it had been a costly flop. For years after that, A.B.C. steered clear of all major sports on television.

The man responsible for moving the network back into college football was a smart young producer named Ed Scherick. After some years with an advertising agency, Scherick formed his own company called "Sports Programs, Inc." and operated it out of a small office on New York's 42nd Street. Ed's right-hand man was a personable young fellow by the name of Chet Simmons, one of the most capable and popular men in our business. He has also been one of the most understanding of all the TV executives. Chet is now director of sports at N.B.C.-TV, where he and the vice president in charge of sports, Carl Lindemann, make a top executive team.

At first, S.P.I. stuck to sport shows of the studio type, but Scherick's real ambition was to televise major events direct from the scenes of action. He developed a close relationship with Tom Moore, then A.B.C.'s vice president in charge of programming. Eventually, Scherick convinced Moore that college football was worth going after again.

To the surprise of everyone in the industry, A.B.C. outbid N.B.C. for the right to televise N.C.A.A. football in 1961 and 1962. The first thing Scherick did was hire for his producer a stout young redhead named Roone Arledge, who had been directing studio shows at N.B.C.

Arledge took the job because he loved sports and wanted to concentrate on them, which he had been unable to do at N.B.C. He turned out to be the hottest sports television producer in the business, and has since become A.B.C.'s vice president in charge of sports programming.

I was next on Scherick's list. He hired me to do the play-by-play, and Paul Christman, Missouri's former All-America quarterback, to do the color. Scherick also signed Bill Bennington, former N.B.C. director of football and the Rose Bowl Parade, as director of the new series.

Bob Neal, Cleveland's colorful sports announcer, joined us to do the sideline broadcasting, including interviews with players and coaches and anything else of interest there. A friend of Scherick's named Charles Howard, who worked in a bank but wanted to get into sports, completed the crew's nucleus as a sort of general assistant to everybody. Although he had only a fan's knowledge of sports, Charlie learned fast and was one of the hardest workers I ever saw. He now produces A.B.C.'s popular "Wide World of Sports."

Arledge wrote and had printed a pamphlet explaining his own ideas on how college football should be televised. His theme was: "Instead of taking the game to the fan, we will take the fan to the game." We would do closeups of players and coaches with miniature shoulder cameras, immediate interviews when players came off the field and reactions of fans in the stands. We would use huge, mobile "shotgun" microphones to pick up the quarterback's signals as he barked them out. We would video-tape the entire game, rerunning highlights of the first half during the intermission and of the second when the game ended.

On my first reading of Arledge's pamphlet my reaction was, "The guy's nuts. How does he think he can pull this off?"

Roone wasn't nuts. He was simply about ten jumps ahead of the competition. He did everything he said he could do, and more. All of the latest improvements in televising football are based on his ideas, including the immediate rerun of video tape so fans can study an important play seconds after it takes place.

We had a production meeting in Birmingham the night before our first telecast, the Alabama-Georgia game of 1961. After Arledge described his elaborate plans for bringing the game to the fan, Christman expressed my own early reaction by asking, "How about the game itself? Will we ever get around to that?"

Of course we were both wrong. Thanks to Roone, we not only did the game, but included all the refinements he wanted.

After the first two games, Arledge made a major improvement. He fired his boss, Ed Sherick, as stage manager up in the booth. With everything he owned riding on the success of these football telecasts, Scherick was a wild man who nearly made nervous wrecks of us all. He yelled like a cheerleader on every play. He jumped up and down when he didn't agree with a decision. He even threw his hat down the way an official tosses his handkerchief when a penalty was called. We had to get him out of the booth before we all went crazy.

"Ed," Roone told him, "stay home. You can help us more watching on your own TV set and telling us what we're doing wrong on Monday."

But Scherick showed up for our third game—Colorado at Kansas—so Arledge conned him into watching it on a TV set in the office of the Kansas chancellor. When it turned out to be a great game and a smooth telecast, Scherick was convinced. After that, he stayed home on Saturdays.

Late every Friday afternoon when we had finished our preparations for the telecast, we had a touch football game. At first we borrowed a ball from the home team, but Roone finally decided we should have our own. Marv Schlenker, one of the assistant directors, had the job of bringing the ball in from New York. I don't know what Arledge would have done to Marv if he ever forgot. Roone took these games pretty seriously.

Christman wouldn't lower himself to play with us, so we made him the referee. He made some pretty bad calls, but we let him keep the job. A local camera crew even filmed one of our games, but I never saw the results.

I depend heavily on coaches for strategy. I've found most are cooperative and accommodating. They're willing to let us sit in on skull sessions, watch their movies, and listen to their instructions and discussions with the boys just before key games.

I had heard that Woody Hayes of Ohio State was temperamental and hard to get along with, but I never found him so. Before a Michigan State game a few years ago, he invited Paul and me to join him and his coaches in a last-minute review of some movies of the opposition. When we asked him if we could interview him between the halves he said, "Look, I'm anxious to sell college football on television. I think it's just as good a show as pro football, and I'll do anything you fellows want me to." With a million other things on his mind, he came on with us for several minutes at halftime.

That same week we spent some time with Duffy Daugherty, the Michigan State coach, who also opened his locker room to us, and let us listen to his strategy sessions and watch his movies while he went over plays with his boys. By the time the game started, Paul and I knew the basic plans of both coaches, the key plays of both teams, and any surprise plays that might come up. It helped us no end in our broadcast.

In 1961 I did the Oklahoma-Army game at Yankee Stadium, one of the big college spectacles of the year. Oklahoma had lost its first five games, but was to win its next five to become one of the nation's powerhouses. On the night before the game I took Roone Arledge up to see Wilkinson to talk about the game and reminisce about old times. Just before we left, I said, "Bud, we want to be sure and do a good game tomorrow. Is there anything for us to look for?"

"Yes," he said. "Somewhere along the line, probably in the second quarter, we're going to pull a no-huddle play on Army. First we'll run a routine play into the middle of the line, and untangle slowly, hoping to catch Army in their defensive huddle. We'll then suddenly line up and snap the ball before Army gets set. The quarterback will lateral it to one of our backs who'll run along our left side convoyed by most of the team. If this works Army will be totally unprepared and we can go for long yardage, maybe a touchdown.

"So during the first half I would advise you not to take the camera off the field too quickly for crowd shots or color or a commercial. We're depending heavily on surprise, but we want to surprise the Army team, not you people."

We were both sworn to secrecy, of course. The next afternoon Roone, working in the video truck, where they decide which shots to use, told the director to keep the camera on the ball after scrimmage plays during the first half.

Sure enough, halfway through the second quarter, Oklahoma pulled the switch, catching Army flat-footed and going seventy yards for a touchdown. Nobody had the play except the television cameras. The movie crews shooting the game for Oklahoma and West Point were in the habit of stopping their cameras after each play to save footage. They were caught as flat-footed as the Army team, and missed the play completely.

11

Fidel Castro loused up plenty of more important things, but one of his lesser sins was his disruption of the greatest light tackle fishing grounds I ever saw. The waters around Cuba are marvelous for fishing of every type, but I think the most fabulous spot of all must be the gorgeous Isle of Pines. It was discovered as a fisherman's paradise by the world's foremost authority on the subject, Joe Brooks, lecturer, author, and the best of good companions. Through Brooks, the Isle of Pines was developed for fishing by a guide named Vic Barothy. Without spoiling the wild beauty of the forest and its waters, Barothy built a camp of incomparable loveliness. Every building, a main lodge and smaller houses of pine, covered with thatched roofs, blended perfectly with the natural surroundings. You didn't have to be a fisherman to enjoy the place. Just in case you were, though, Barothy had four houseboats for overnight trips around the island.

The Isle of Pines, off the southern coast of Cuba and about a half hour by air from Havana, had originally been the site of a prison. Outside of a small town and an air-strip, the island was unspoiled, and Joe Brooks fell in love with it. So did Barothy when Joe took him there. Vic had been working off the Florida Keys, but wanted to leave because of its growing commercialism. With Brooks' encouragement, Barothy hired a crew to build his camp, which he opened for business in the early fifties.

Brooks raved about the place for some time before he sold me on it. The clincher was Joe's insistence that it was just as enjoyable for women as for men. Jerre took a dim view of fishing trips. Every time I took her on one she ended up stuck in a cabin or a hotel room waiting for me. When I first told her about the Isle of Pines she had the usual so-what reaction. She weakened when I relayed Brooks' assurance that it was a great place for women, and finally agreed to go when I told her Joe was taking his wife, Mary.

In January of 1956, Jerre and I flew to Miami where we met the Brookses and two of Joe's innumerable fisherman friends. One was Count Etienne de Ganay of Paris, the other a Mr. Dennison, part owner of the Dennison-Johnson Spinning Reel Company. Joe knew lots of princes and dukes and counts and was quite at home with this one, but it took Jerre and me a little time to get used to real, live, on-the-level nobility. It wasn't too difficult, for the count was a great guy who soon put us at our ease.

We flew to Havana and from there to the Isle of Pines where Barothy and his wife met us. A blocky man with sandy hair and blue eyes, Vic greeted us with a roar you could hear the length of the airport, hugging Joe in the Latin-American fashion, although he was no more Latin-American than we were. Mrs. Barothy was close to forty, but you'd never know it. Stunningly beautiful, she had brown eyes and brown hair, the figure of a chorus girl, the brains of a savant, and the charm of a child. She came from the States and, although she loved the island, went to New York once a year to catch up on new Broadway shows. Jerre was a theater buff herself, and she and Mrs. Barothy soon became good friends.

Our first stop was Cookie's bar in town. Cookie, a short, black-haired Cuban with a lush mustache that drooped at the ends, was Barothy's closest buddy. They greeted each other as if they hadn't met in twenty years, although we found out later they were together practically every day. The two kept up a running fire of gags, stories, and friendly insults, stopping only to howl at each other's jokes. Although we didn't understand everything that went on

because they switched back and forth between English
and Spanish, we howled with them, for the warmth of
their good fellowship was infectious.

It was about half an hour's drive from town to the lodge,
where we had more cocktails and a fine dinner, then went
to bed in one of the little thatched-roof houses. The rustling
of tall pines in a gentle breeze lulled us to a sleep interrupted only by a call at seven in the morning. We were to
leave on one of the houseboats at eight.

A huge native—about six feet four inches tall—fixed us a
marvelous breakfast of tropical fruits, bacon and eggs,
coffee, and the lightest, most delicious honey cakes I ever
tasted. This man cooked with the touch of a master chef,
and we were delighted to see him go aboard the houseboat
as a member of the crew. Mrs. Barothy stayed behind, but
Vic came as captain and chief guide. We towed two fishing
skiffs, and had a guide for each. The houseboat had only
two staterooms, but that was all we needed. Jerre and
Mary Brooks used one and the count and Mr. Dennison the
other. The rest of us slept on the deck.

"We're going to a place I've never seen myself," Barothy
said. "It's southeast of here and will take us about thirteen
hours towing the skiffs. Some of the places we'll fish have
never been fished before, and I'm told they're fabulous."

We sailed all day, moving very slowly on a clear blue
surface, warm and beautiful but as smooth as an ice rink.
By suppertime we were on the opposite side of the island
from the lodge.

"There'll be a pretty stiff wind at eight," Vic told us. "It
comes every night. You never know how long it will last—
maybe an hour, maybe four. You didn't notice it last night
because we were on land."

The night wind, as Barothy called it, came up promptly
at eight, and it was pretty nearly a gale that night. The boat
rocked so much I got a bit woozy. One of the fishing skiffs
was torn loose and we had to go back for it in the dark. The

wind didn't let up for hours, so we anchored out to sea, and came in to make camp the next morning.

We had a wonderful week, fishing and exploring the little islands, visiting spots few if any people had ever visited before. We fished mostly in the flats, only two or three feet deep, so clear that we could see all manner of creatures swimming and crawling about. There were bonefish, the most timid fish in the world, and baby tarpon, and snook and lemon sharks, and starfish, and land crabs, and snails, and little barracuda. Every morning the big native cook told us to be sure to bring back some barracuda. They were his own favorite food and he fixed them up so fluffy they melted in your mouth like his wonderful honey cakes.

One morning Joe and I got eighteen bonefish on artificial flies. The most I've ever heard of anyone catching at one stretch. But these fish had never seen artificial lures before, or, for that matter, any kind of lures. Fish are not as stupid as they sometimes look. The next day we caught fewer bonefish and fewer still the day after that. We could see them, but they knew we were there and weren't so quick to rise to our bait.

We came back to camp for lunch every day, and then at five in the afternoon for drinks and dinner. Sand flies came out at early evening, but they were gone by nightfall when we went out to fish for tarpon. We caught them as big as forty pounds. The only trouble was the lemon sharks were out then, too, so you'd be lucky to reel in a tarpon that hadn't been picked to pieces. One night Joe Brooks hooked a big tarpon and fought the fish for fifteen minutes before his line went slack. All he brought in was a head.

One day Vic took us into an old charcoal ditch. We went through a canal so narrow and thick with branches that we had to duck our heads in the skiff. We traveled maybe a mile and came out on a little pearl of a lake, no bigger than a couple of city blocks. It was loaded with lily pads in bloom and everywhere we looked baby tarpons up to thirty pounds were coming up for air and rolling around.

"There are snook here, too," Barothy said. "Millions of them."

Snook is a real delicacy, a tropical game fish around Florida and Caribbean waters. It's also called salt water pike. It has a stripe running down its side and many of the characteristics of tarpon, for it's a tremendous game fish and a real fighter. So many snook were caught around Florida that the supply became depleted, and the State stopped commercial fishermen from taking them in nets. They live in the ocean, but they like to go up ditches and brackish water lakes like the one Vic led us to that day.

We had a picnic. Even Jerre, who isn't the world's greatest fisherwoman, got her share of baby tarpon and snook. They weren't very easy to miss. They were all over the place.

On the fourth day out we were in our camp for lunch when we saw a speck on the horizon. Since leaving Barothy's lodge we had seen a total of three boats, all Cuban sailboats. But as the speck grew larger we realized this was a big power yacht.

"Oh, oh," Vic said. "I guess it's the old man."

"Who's the old man?" I asked.

"Batista."

Pretty soon the yacht dropped anchor and, after some waving back and forth, a motor launch came toward us. Barothy got in and went out to the yacht on it. After lunch with the President of Cuba Vic came back, the yacht went on its way, and we resumed our fishing.

"How do you know Batista?" I asked Barothy later.

"He likes to fish."

"Have you taken him out?"

"A few times."

"What's he like?"

"Nice fellow," Vic said.

That was all I could get out of him.

Whatever Batista may or may not have been, he encouraged sports in general, and was glad to welcome Barothy to Cuba. Castro wasted little time driving Vic out. His men took over the Isle of Pines, and the Barothys were lucky to escape with their lives. They left with two of their trusted employees—I always wondered if one was that native cook—and made their way to Miami. They lost everything they owned, but friends set them up in another camp off British Honduras. Vic claims the fishing is even better than the Isle of Pines, which I find hard to believe.

Ever since that trip I've wanted to do a fishing broadcast. I talked about it often with Roone Arledge as a possibility for A.B.C.'s "Wide World of Sports" program, but we couldn't figure out how to insert the element of competition, an integral part of the show. Mort Neff, producer of a highly successful outdoor sports program in Detroit, came up with the answer. He suggested going to Argentina for a world's championship trout fishing contest. I flipped when Roone told me about it. I wanted to go, and I knew Joe Brooks would be delighted. He had made many trips to the Argentine, and had written some great stories about the fantastic trout fishing there.

Among his worldwide fishing friends were Bebe Anchorina and Jorge Donovan, both wealthy Argentinian ranch owners.

Five of us left New York to fly to Miami in February of 1962. Besides Joe, Roone, and me, there were Bob Wood, who would be director and chief cameraman, and Lenny Lencina, who would handle the sound. Mort met us in Miami, from where we took off on a thirteen-hour flight to Buenos Aires. There we were met by Bebe and Jorge, who had driven a little matter of six hundred miles to be there. Anchorina was small and dark, with perfectly groomed jet black hair, bright, alert eyes and a polite, gentlemanly manner. Donovan was a huge man who looked as Irish as his name, although his family had lived in the Argentine for several generations.

We left Buenos Aires the next day in a prop plane for Bariloche, some 840 miles to the southwest. The plane made five stops, each scheduled for fifteen minutes, but Argentina, in common with the rest of Latin America, is full of people with plenty of time. Nobody, including airline pilots, is in a hurry. We hung around each airport over an hour, slaking our thirst with beer or soft drinks while waiting for takeoff. I learned the reason for the delays from an English-speaking attendant at the first stop.

Half an hour after we were scheduled to leave I asked him when we would go.

"We're waiting for a passenger," he said.

"One passenger?"

"We can't disappoint him. He depends on us to get him where he's going."

"Why not insist he be here on time?"

The man shrugged. "He'll be here," he said. "We phoned and he told us he'd be a little late."

That happened all along the way. The passengers ran the airline.

Bariloche is a breathtakingly beautiful replica of a Swiss village. A lovely town built where the mountains meet a lake, it looked as if it had been picked up and lifted right out of the Alps and set down, houses, buildings, streets, and all, right in the Andes. The homes are Swiss chalets, the buildings gabled and latticed, with odd-shaped doors and windows and gingerbread decor.

The town is one of the most popular year-round resorts in the Argentine, with skiing and skating and sledding and tobogganing in the winter and fishing, boating, hiking, and swimming in the summer. Since the seasons are the reverse of ours, we arrived there on a crowded midsummer's day. We wouldn't have been able to stay if reservations had not been made for us several weeks in advance.

We spent a night and the better part of the following day in Bariloche, then flew over a high mountain range and into the Pampas to the town of Esquel, about 120 miles south of Bariloche. It was there that we joined our opponents in the world's championship trout fishing contest. The men whom producer Mort Neff had picked to represent Argentina in the "Wide World of Sports" show were Tito Hosman, a wealthy lawyer from Buenos Aires, and Erick Gornik, an outfitter and guide who lived in Esquel. Both were big, bluff, hearty men who greeted us with Argentine bear hugs, and I knew immediately that, win, lose, or draw, we were going to have a wonderful time.

Gornik, a tall man with crystal blue eyes, blond hair, and a well-manicured beard, had a rich, resonant voice which would have made him a fortune on the stage, television, or the lecture platform. I don't know how many other languages he could speak but he was fluent in Spanish, German, French, Norwegian, and English. His English accent was odd, and he added "gee" to almost everything he said. "He's a nice fellow-gee," or "That's a big mountain-gee," or "Look at the size of that fish-gee," were typical Gornik expressions. Before he was through, he had us all doing it. To this day, when I go fishing with any of the boys who were in the Argentine with me, I say, "Isn't that a beauty-gee?" when we land a big fish.

Hosman, a dead ringer for Ernest Hemingway, was just as impressive in appearance and speech. A barrel-chested six-footer with a big white beard and twinkling dark eyes, he fractured the English language with a British accent acquired at Oxford. Everything was "miserable"—"Let's try that miserable lake again," or "I'll have another miserable cup of tea"—and he prefaced almost all his remarks in English with, "See here, old chap." I guess he was as multilingual as Gornik because the two swung easily from one language to another, telling jokes in all of them and roaring

with laughter in that universal language everyone under-
stands.

Our "Wide World of Sports" fishing contest was to be
held on Lago General Paz, a big lake on the Argentine-
Chile border three hundred miles from Esquel and only
four hundred miles north of Tierra del Fuego, at the southern tip of the continent. The only way to get there was
by car over terrain much like our own West. Some of the
trip was through the Pampas, the great plains of South
America, the rest over or around towering mountains on
narrow, winding gravel roads with frightening drops if you
missed a turn. With two trucks and two jeeps, it would be
a twelve-hour trip. Gornik's men were loading the trucks
in the back yard of his home when we arrived from Bariloche. We were to travel in a jeep driven by Don MacArthur,
a Panagra Airways pilot who was a good friend of Mort
Neff and knew Argentina.

We didn't get away from Esquel until four in the afternoon. I knew the driving through the mountains would be
tough, but I thought the roads across the Pampas would be
just like our roads at home. They weren't. There wasn't a
pavement anywhere—just endless stretches of dusty, bumpy,
rut-filled gravel road. As we jounced along, my back began
bothering me, but I had brought along pain pills for just
such a contingency. I must have used up half of them on
the trip.

We were still on the road when it got dark, and Gornik
said, "This isn't good. We should have arrived before nightfall. We'll have to eat in Rio Pico."

Rio Pico, with a population of about three hundred, was
the biggest town between Esquel and Lago General Paz.
We drove up in front of a ratty building called the Rio
Pico Hosteria, and I really gulped when we walked inside.

"You guys can eat here if you want to, but not me," I
said. "This is the filthiest joint I've ever seen."

"Never mind what it looks like," Joe said. "They've got

food and we're starved. You can wait for us out in the jeep if you want."

I looked around and decided to stay with the crowd. The customers were mean-looking gauchos who glared at us as if they were measuring our throats. Two had jagged scars down the sides of their cheeks.

The manager, bearing the worst-looking scar of all—from temple to chin—came out and embraced Gornik and Hosman. The three of them chattered happily away while the rest of us sat at the bar. I was famished, but didn't dare order anything except a beer, which I drank out of the bottle after carefully wiping off the top with a handkerchief. At around ten o'clock Erick came over and said, "All right, boys, we're ready for dinner."

We went into a room in back, with a big table beautifully set. When we sat down a lovely woman with olive skin and black hair flecked with gray, and wearing a spotless white dress and white gaucho boots, came out. She was the manager's wife. In excellent English she said, "Good evening, gentlemen. I think you'll enjoy the dinner we have for you. I'm sorry I didn't have more time to prepare it."

She brought in steaming hot barley soup, so good I had three bowls of it.

"For a guy who wouldn't eat you're doing pretty well," Roone remarked.

"Well," I said, "it's all I'm going to have."

But then the lady in white came in with heaping bowls of lettuce and huge ruby red tomatoes, so I had several helpings of that.

"I thought you were going to stop with the soup," Joe said.

"That salad looked too good," I said. "But now I'm through."

The next course was rare beef, sliced in pieces so thin you could see through them, and topped with eggs. I must have had a dozen helpings. Finally, in came caramel pudding, the Argentine national dessert, and a caramel cheese that melted like butter in your mouth. I stuffed myself with both, washing everything down with the most delicious coffee I ever tasted.

As I practically staggered back through that bar and out into the jeep, Joe Brooks said, "Curt, if you get the Argentine trots, don't blame me."

"The hell with the Argentine trots," I replied. "That was the greatest meal I ever ate."

It was nearly midnight when we left Rio Pico, but we had to push on through to the lake because there was nowhere else to stay. We skirted a forest fire on the way, and at about two-thirty in the morning arrived at a lumber camp barred by locked gates. Gornik hiked down to wake up the owner, a German with a squeaky voice. He opened the place and led us to our bunks. Joe and I ended up in an old shed with one bed. Joe climbed into that and I slept on the floor, since my back hurt from the long, bumpy ride.

We were awakened at dawn. After breakfast we set out on the one-mile walk to Lago General Paz. We were still five hundred feet above the lake when we caught our first glimpse of it. What a picture! The bluest blue water I've ever seen nestled in a framework of snow-capped peaks. The lake looked like a tremendous sapphire set in a ring of huge pearls. For a minute none of us moved; we simply stood and stared at this breathtaking sight.

"Good heavens!" somebody said. "Is that real?"

"You'll see," Erick answered. "And in that beautiful lake are the biggest, most beautiful trout in the world."

"The water looks cold," I said.

"It is. The mean temperature is 48 degrees."

Erick told us our contest would be on the Chilean side of the lake, working out of an abandoned lumber camp there. We would travel back and forth by skiff. He had arranged this with both the Argentine and Chilean governments, but an Argentine forest ranger ruined the plan. He came around as we were getting ready to leave, insisting that if we crossed the frontier we couldn't get back. All the arguments that Erick, Tito, and Don MacArthur could muster failed to budge the man at first. He finally agreed to let us fish the Chilean side if we set up our camp on the Argentine side. That meant finding a new base and traveling an extra hour each way every day by boat, but we had no choice. We had come over six thousand miles for a fishing contest and it would have to be on the ranger's terms or not at all.

We started out in one of the boats to look for a camp within reasonable distance of the contest fishing grounds and still in Argentina. The lake wasn't as pretty to travel on as to look at. The winds came howling down from the mountains, bouncing the skiffs around like corks, so we had a rough ride. We found a fairly protected beach and inlet on the far side of the lake, but there was no cover whatever. After a couple of frantic days of running back and forth for our gear and a couple of freezing nights in sleeping bags, we began to get organized. The men built a few shacks, set up a kitchen, made some rough furniture, and cut trails—which Gornik named the Gowdy Trail and the Brooks Trail—from the camp to the beach.

With all the camera and sound equipment loaded on the skiffs, we looked like the *Mutiny on the Bounty* movie set when we headed for the contest grounds. Roone Arledge, Mort Neff, Bob Wood, and Lenny Lencina took over to make sure of the best spots for television sound and pictures and to get everything set up. That took several more days. It was a week after our arrival at Lago General Paz before the contest finally started.

The ground rules called for one day of fishing with spinning rods, the second day with fly rods, and the third day open. We would get one point per pound for every trout we caught, with a bonus to the man who reeled in the biggest fish of the day. The world's championship would be won by the team with the highest combined total after three days of fishing.

The toughest problem was setting the contest up so that everyone had a fair chance to fish in the best waters. Each of us would fish with an opponent, usually Tito with me and Erick with Joe. One pair would go to one spot and the other to another. After an hour we would swap places.

Another problem was that, although we had two cameramen, Bob Wood and Mort Neff, Lenny Lencina was our only sound man. That meant we couldn't fish too far apart because he had to be within hailing distance so he could go back and forth with a battery-run tape recorder to get all the sounds and conversation when anyone caught anything.

It was hard for Roone Arledge, who was referee and timekeeper as well as producer, to make sure we all had a full hour of fishing. Whenever somebody made a catch, everything had to stop while the fish was weighed and photographed. If the lighting wasn't right, pictures would have to be taken from different angles, and that would cut into fishing time. Thus, while one pair might have a full hour of actual fishing, the other might have only three-quarters of an hour. Roone had to make adjustments so that both pairs would have the same amount of time in the same places.

Fishing was further slowed by the cameramen, both of whom had to do a lot of running around and splashing through the water. Every time that happened, the fish scattered and it took awhile for them to return to where they had been before.

Since the contest depended on the size of the fish, weighing them was important. Brooks had brought along a small scale designed for the purpose and recognized as official by most sporting organizations. The trouble was the fish had to be killed for weighing, and we didn't want to kill every fish we caught. We wanted to be sportsmen, and show on television that every fish except those for eating should be released.

We solved that problem by making educated guesses. After the first day we could tell within a few ounces a fish's weight without putting him on the scale. If both sides agreed, that was how the weight was recorded, and after getting pictures we threw the fish back into the water. The only exceptions were when somebody caught a real whopper or, as on the last day, when the contest was so close practically every ounce counted.

Arledge was a bear for getting live sound. He didn't want the show to be a travelogue with the narration dubbed in later in New York. He insisted that Lencina get close to us with his tape recorder so all the talk would be genuine.

This caused some argument because Lenny had no waders and couldn't stand the 46-degree temperature without them. Believe me, it was cold enough even with waders and heavy pants. Lencina just about congealed every time he came out into the water to catch what we were saying. We finally had to patch up an old pair of waders that Gornik had in his luggage, and Lencina got around in them.

He was very clever at placing mikes where they would do the most good. We fished near the shore, so he put them under bushes, behind logs, on the ground near rocks —anywhere they would be protected from the wind that howled down the mountains and over the lake. In this way, he could get the actual sounds of the scene, the struggling fish splashing in the water, the whip of the rods, the sounds of the reels, and other immediate and pertinent noises. At the same time, he could screen out much of the wind, which was interfering with the sounds Lenny wanted to reproduce. For our own voices, we all wore small mikes beneath our shirts.

Wood and Lencina had a hard time keeping the equipment in shape. It was about an hour's ride over the rough windswept lake from our camp to the fishing site, and they didn't dare leave any of that valuable stuff at the scene. For one thing, it might get lost. For another, we couldn't fish on successive days because of the weather and it might be damaged if left untended for more than a few hours.

So we had to load everything in the skiffs and haul it back and forth every time we went out. This was especially hazardous on the return trip when the whitecapped waves tossed us around as if we were in the middle of the ocean. The boats were loaded to the gunwales, and we were always afraid something would fall overboard or a boat would tip.

No matter how careful we were, we couldn't keep the delicate electronic equipment dry. Night after night, Wood and Lencina worked by battery-run lanterns in a little wooden shed to get the moisture out of the cameras and the tape recorder.

Despite the perils, the isolation, the primitive living conditions, the delays, and the long trips from camp to contest and back, Wood and Neff got remarkable pictures and Lencina sharp, clear sound. Everything was in color, in perfect focus, and the scenery was caught with such stark realism that when I saw the show later I could feel the icy water and gasp at the grandeur of the snow-capped mountains.

The contest itself was interesting, but anticlimactic. The important thing was to bring to American audiences a magnificent segment of South American outdoor sports life. We were only the backdrop. The central figures were the beauties of nature in strange surroundings, which few American viewers would ever see except on television.

I got off to a bad start because I've always been a better fly than a spinning fisherman. After a while I realized I was working my lures too quickly. The others were putting brook trout in with slow-moving wobbly lures, and I was working my wobbler too fast. Joe and the Argentines began hauling in fish before I did, and they got some beauties. The fish ran four to six pounds, and had the loveliest coloring I've ever seen on brook trout. The water temperature and the fresh water shrimp on which the fish fed both contributed to these magnificent shadings. The trout fishing in that lake was the finest I ever saw anywhere. I finally began pulling in my share of fish, but it was Joe who kept us from being murdered by the two Argentines. At the end of the first day Erick and Tito, with fifty-four points, were ten ahead of us.

We couldn't go out for the second leg of the contest for four days. We spent the time reading, playing chess, checking over our gear, or just talking. Erick and Tito were marvelously entertaining, and it was impossible to be bored with them. We all had stories and gags to swap, so the time passed quickly despite the long delay.

On the second day of fishing, this time with fly rods, I did much better, but the Argentines continued to move ahead of us. Despite a seven-pounder that gave us the bonus points for the biggest fish, we lost by nine points that time, and were nineteen behind for the first two days combined.

Joe gave me a pep talk the night before our last day out. "Curt," he said, "remember, this is going to be on nationwide television. Won't we look great if we get our brains beaten out again! I didn't come these six thousand miles to lose, and neither did you. Tomorrow, let's fish every cast out, take our time, and not panic."

At his insistence we used spinning rods. The water was very deep, so flies took too long to reach them. Spinning lures made it much faster, and with the score 104 to 85 against us, we couldn't afford to waste a minute. When we started out on the last morning I left my fly equipment behind.

Tito and I fished together that day, and he elected to use a fly rod. I had a hot morning and pulled in four four- or five-pounders in a row while Tito caught only one. We were back in the fishing contest. With the end coming at four in the afternoon, it was touch and go for the rest of the way. Joe settled the issue only ten minutes before the finish when he pulled in a six-pounder that gave us a 136–130 victory.

On the way back to Bariloche from Lago General Paz, our jeep suddenly went out of control. Don MacArthur was going about fifty miles an hour when the steering wheel came off. We careened all over the dusty highway as Don frantically tried to jam the wheel back on while throttling down our speed. We went off the road, but the drop at that point was only forty feet. As we slid down I thought surely we'd turn over, but the jeep kept its wheels, and we finally came to rest without anyone suffering a scratch. A truck came by half an hour later. The driver lent Don some tools so he could get the steering wheel back on, and we went on our way.

So we were nearly arrested, nearly killed in an accident, nearly drowned and nearly frozen to death in ice-cold water, but it was one of the most thrilling experiences of my life.

I'd do it again any time. All I need is an excuse.

12

Except for Ted Williams, the greatest student of baseball I ever saw was Dom DiMaggio. Overshadowed by his brother Joe and handicapped by his pedestrian appearance, Dom never got the credit he deserved. With his comparatively short stature and his thick glasses, he hardly looked the part of a ballplayer, but he was a great one. He could run and throw and field fully as well as Joe, but of course he lacked Joe's power and remarkable magnetism.

Not that Dom didn't have power. He had plenty, and every so often belted one out of the ball park. However, his appearance was very deceptive. He looked like nine million other guys in street clothes, and in uniform as well. But stripped to the waist, he looked every inch the fine athlete that he was. He had the wide shoulders and huge chest of a heavyweight boxer, arms that were thick and muscular, and a body that tapered down in the classic mold of physical perfection.

He was the only player I ever knew who consistently sat in the dugout to watch the opposing team in batting practice. He wanted to know if good hitters were swinging in their normal groove and if there was anything unusual to expect. Dom never took his eyes off a ballplayer he had never seen before. As Williams studied pitchers to know how to hit them, Dom DiMaggio studied hitters to know how to play them.

In the spring of 1953 he had an eye operation. By the time he was ready to play, a rookie named Tommy Umphlett was in center field for the Red Sox and hitting like mad. Manager Lou Boudreau refused to bench or shift the kid, and Dom refused to sit on the bench. Dom's premature retirement turned out a blessing in disguise. He went into the manufacturing business in Lawrence, Massachusetts, and is now the highly successful proprietor of a plant employing several hundred people. Among his other financial interests is a part ownership of the Boston Patriots football team.

The Red Sox haven't won any pennants since I've been with them, but they have had more than their share of interesting, unusual characters. One of the most amazing was Jim Piersall, the only big league ballplayer to come back after a mental breakdown requiring shock treatments and intensive psychiatric care. Piersall's story is well known through his book and movie, *Fear Strikes Out*.

I first saw Piersall at spring training in 1952. A twenty-two-year-old product of our farm system, he was a handsome, high-strung, eager kid with fiery brown eyes, jet black hair, and a huge smile. He brimmed over with vitality and energy, and constantly drew attention to himself with his loud, rapid-fire talk and his too obvious apprehension about his baseball future. For some reason or other, he seemed most fearful of knuckleball pitchers. He talked about them constantly.

He started on me one day as we were sitting on the bench at the ball park in Sarasota.

"I can't hit knucklers, Curt," he said. "What am I going to do?"

Vern Stephens happened to be on the other side of me. "Let me tell you something, kid," he said, leaning over in front of me. "You can't worry about one specific pitch. If you do, you're not going to make it up here. You've got to have confidence in yourself."

"Besides," I added, "there are only a couple of guys in the whole league who can get knucklers over the plate. You won't see them ten times all season."

But nobody could talk Piersall out of his obsession about knucklers. None of us realized that what really worried him was his shift from the outfield to shortstop. In his troubled mental state, he interpreted that to mean the Red Sox didn't want him at all. He thought they intended to get rid of him, that they knew he couldn't make it as a shortstop and would use his failure as an excuse to send him back to the minors.

If manager Lou Boudreau had had the slightest indication of what was going through Piersall's mind he would never have shifted the youngster. Actually, Boudreau needed a shortstop badly and thought Piersall, a remarkable outfielder, would make a great one. Jim started the season at short and did very well, although he became harder and harder to handle. He battled umpires, got into fights, mocked other ballplayers, clowned during games, played up to the fans, and made himself conspicuous in any number of other ways.

I thought this was all because of his intense desire to make good, and so did most others, I suppose. I had him on the air a few times, and he was wonderful. The sight of a microphone seemed to have a soothing effect on him. He talked lucidly and well, his diction was good, and he had interesting things to say.

One day at Fenway Park I was standing in the dugout next to where the day's lineup was pasted on the wall. Boudreau had decided to rest Piersall, and had somebody else down for shortstop. When Jim saw that his name was missing, he spat all over the lineup card and began to cry.

"I knew Boudreau didn't like me," he said. "He doesn't want me on the ball club."

"Don't be ridiculous, Jim," I said. "He has nothing against you."

"Aw, don't give me that. He hates me. They all hate me around here."

It was pretty obvious that Piersall had emotional problems, but we still didn't realize how serious they were. Later, after Boudreau returned Jim to the outfield, the Red Sox had a wild ball game with the old St. Louis Browns. The Browns were in front in the ninth inning, with Satchel Paige, ancient but still effective, pitching. Piersall got on base, and staged the funniest show I ever saw on a ball field. He jumped up and down, scratched himself like an ape, waddled like a duck, and yelled at Paige. Nobody in the ball park had ever seen such a performance. It was so unusual, so off-beat, so unexpected that it caught fans, writers, players, umpires, broadcasters, everybody, completely by surprise. First came ripples, then waves of laughter as Piersall persisted in plaguing Paige with his unconventional antics. The ancient pitcher said later that it didn't bother him, but I'm sure it did because he walked three or four men and finally blew the game when Sammy White hit a grand slam home run.

But it was Piersall's game. He had everyone in the ball park laughing. At one point I was roaring so hard I had to turn the microphone over to Bob DeLaney, my broadcasting partner, who was having his own troubles trying to keep from breaking up. The next day the newspapers were full of Piersall's capers. White, the man who won the game with his grand slam, didn't rate more than a couple of lines at the bottom of all the stories.

Joe Cronin told me that it was Piersall's behavior that night which convinced the Red Sox he might need medical attention. Some weeks later, he was sent to the Westboro State Hospital, a mental institution west of Boston, apparently finishing a promising career before it got fairly started. But Jim then made his amazing comeback to become one of the greatest outfielders in baseball history. I saw him make some unbelievable catches.

Some people disliked Piersall because of his tremendous drive, but I always got along very well with him. He was smart and publicity-conscious, an excellent speaker and a hard worker. His one bad fault was an obsession about money, which caused jealousy and unrest among the other ballplayers in his later years with the Red Sox.

He had a poor year in 1958, his last in Boston. While I was sitting with him on a bus coming back from a night game in Kansas City just before the season ended, he pulled a little black book from his pocket and started writing in it.

"What's that for?" I asked.

"I had two line drives that were caught tonight," he said. "I keep track of these things for when I go in to talk about my new contract."

"You mean you're going to ask for more money? Why, you're only hitting about .240."

"I'd be hitting .300 if some of those line drives had dropped in safely."

"How about the bloop hits you got?" I asked. "Do you keep track of those, too?"

He shook his head. "Those are base hits," he said. "I don't have to keep track of them."

"So you're going to hit Cronin for a raise on the basis of the bloop hits you got and the line drive hits you didn't get?"

"Not a big raise," Jim said. "Just a little one. Then maybe he won't cut me for the lousy year I had."

The Red Sox didn't cut him. They just traded him to Cleveland.

Ellis Kinder was another remarkable character. At forty Kinder was the best relief pitcher in the American League. In his thirties when he came into the majors, Ellis made his own training rules and strictly adhered to them.

We got on the train for Cleveland one night in Chicago, and a few of us, including Boudreau and Kinder, headed for the club car for a nightcap. At midnight, Boudreau, who was drinking Cokes, said, "All right, fellows, let's go. We've got a tough doubleheader tomorrow."

Everyone but Kinder got up and left. Lou looked at him and said, "How about it, Ellie?"

"Goodnight, Skip," Kinder said. "Pleasant dreams."

He didn't move and neither did Boudreau. The waiter came around and Lou ordered another Coke. Kinder pointed to his own glass and said, "The same."

"The same as him?" the waiter asked.

"No," said Kinder. "The same as I had before."

After a while Boudreau said, "Well, Ellie, big day tomorrow. What do you think?"

"I think you ought to go to bed, Skip. It's getting late."

"How about you?"

"I'll be along," Kinder said. "Goodnight."

Lou and I left him there.

I don't think he got to bed that night. We arrived in Cleveland at seven the next morning on one of the hottest days I can remember. Even at that hour it was 98. As we got off the train, DeLaney nudged me and said, "Look."

A couple of porters were handing Kinder from train to platform like a sack of potatoes. When they finally got him settled in a wheelchair, his head was rolling around as though on a swivel. As Bob and I rode to the hotel in a cab I said, "We won't see him for a week."

The thermometer was up to about 103 when the first game of the doubleheader started. Maurice McDermott had a no-hitter going for the Red Sox for five or six innings. In the seventh, he finally wilted in the heat, filling the bases with nobody out, and Boudreau had to yank him.

For the second time that day, DeLaney nudged me and said, "Look." And for the second time that day he wanted me to see Ellis Kinder. Only this time Kinder was ambling leisurely out of the bullpen, the perfect picture of the great relief pitcher he was.

He proved it by getting out of the inning without allowing a run. Then he retired the Indians in order in the eighth and ninth to save McDermott's victory.

After the game Boudreau told him, "Ellie, that was the greatest comeback I ever saw. Take a shower, go on back to the hotel, order a couple of beers, and relax."

"I'll stick around, Skip," Kinder said. "I got nowhere to go."

He went back out to the bullpen and later pitched five more innings of shutout ball to save the second game, too.

By 1955 the years finally caught up with him. He struggled along, but the magic was gone from his arm and opposing hitters no longer found him a puzzle. One day late in the season Hank Bauer and Yogi Berra beat him with tremendous homers in the same inning at Yankee Stadium. After the game I ran into Kinder's wife waiting for him outside the players' entrance.

"What do you suppose is the matter with him, Curt?" she asked. "He hasn't had a drink in weeks."

"Maybe that's what's the matter with him," I said.

McDermott was another real character. He had a million-dollar arm and ten-cent judgment, for he couldn't tear himself away from bright lights at small hours of the morning. Sound baseball men shuddered at this flagrant waste of talent, because Maury might have been one of the great southpaws of all time. In his early years with the ball club he lived with Ruth and Johnny Pesky at their home in nearby Lynn. Pesky was a Red Sox infielder at the time. He and his wife alternately pleaded and scolded to make the kid behave. McDermott was always contrite, always promising to be a good boy, but I guess it was too much to ask. Training rules were not for him.

He never had a twenty-game-winning season, but he pitched some marvelous ball games. He once faced twenty-seven men beating the Senators on a one-hitter. The man who got the hit went out in a double play, and nobody else reached. McDermott had no-hitters for five or six innings several times but couldn't keep them going. At other times he looked terrible, getting his brains beaten out in the first or second inning.

Although it never showed in the record books because relief pitchers got credit for extra-inning victories in games that McDermott started, I think his best year was 1951. He went ten or more innings several times, leaving with the games still tied. Once he lasted fifteen innings against Cleveland, but the Red Sox didn't win until the sixteenth and by then McDermott was in the showers.

His greatest performance that year was an incredible seventeen innings against the White Sox in Chicago, in which he gave up only eight hits and two runs. He had nothing to show for that either. The Red Sox lost it in the nineteenth. That was part of the most exciting four-game series I ever broadcast. Every game in it was decided by one run, and not one was settled until the last inning. The Red Sox won three of them.

McDermott's marathon performance came the day after a twi-night doubleheader that started at 6 P.M. The second game went seventeen innings and ended around three in the morning, which was four on the East Coast. With the Red Sox in the thick of the pennant race, thousands of New England fans stayed up to listen right to the bitter end. The electric company later reported that that night their customers used the highest number of kilowatt hours in history for that hour of the morning. A Northeast Airlines pilot said that so many houses had lights on north of Boston that it seemed like New Year's Eve in July. The first thing he asked on landing in Bangor was how the ball game came out.

The star of that doubleheader and the other games in the series was a normally nondescript outfielder named Clyde Vollmer, who was in the midst of the most amazing batting streak I ever heard of. Others may have had more hits or piled up higher averages in a one-month stretch, but no one ever won as many games with key hits at psychological moments. Day after day "Dutch the Clutch" came through in the ninth inning or later to rescue the Red Sox from sure defeat. Sometimes a Vollmer homer tied the score, sometimes a Vollmer single drove in the winning run, and always, it seemed, a Vollmer hit of some kind was the most important blow of the ball game. The month of July 1951, belonged to Vollmer as no single month has ever belonged to a major league ballplayer before or since.

The odd thing was that Vollmer was just a pretty good right-handed batter and an outfielder of no particular consequence. He had played for the Reds and the Senators without causing the lift of a baseball eyebrow, and the Red Sox hardly expected more than occasional pinch-hitting duties from him. When his bat caught fire manager Steve O'Neill played him every day, of course. But by early August Vollmer ran out of hits and that was the end of his dream streak. He didn't seem to mind. A phlegmatic, good-natured man of few words, he could take his base hits or leave them alone.

Frank Sullivan, a huge, gangling pitcher with blond hair and a rubber face, had a great sense of humor. He loved to turn his cap to one side, cross his eyes, make a face like Frank Fontaine, and walk around the field knock-kneed. A six-foot six-inch giant who was all arms and legs on the mound and a real good pitcher for several years, Sully had more brains than balance. He was clever, and had a variety of interests, but you never knew what he was going to do next.

He jumped from fad to fad, from gimmick to gimmick, from deal to deal. He was always going to make a million bucks on some wild scheme, but nothing ever materialized. Whether it was a deal or a gadget or a pastime, he threw himself into it heart and soul. Sully never did things half-way.

He once went absolutely nuts about chess. He carried a couple of sets with him, read all the books he could find on the subject, and badgered other men on the ball club to let him teach them the game. If he found a chess player on another ball club he insisted on a match. If he couldn't get anyone else to play, he set up the board and played against himself. He became pretty good, but finally dropped the game for lack of support and, I suppose, loss of interest.

One night at the Del Prado Hotel in Chicago I woke up in a cold sweat. I thought I heard people hoarsely whispering the names of colors—blue—red—yellow—green—but it was three o'clock in the morning. However, instead of the nightmare I was sure I had, this turned out to be the real thing. Guys really were hoarsely whispering colors in the room next door. When I realized it was Sully's room, I put on a bathrobe and went over to see what was going on.

Sully had the floor cleared and all the chairs and small tables piled up on the bed and dresser to make room for an electric auto racing game. Half the ball club was there betting dollars on different cars which Sully operated by remote control. It must have been five in the morning before we all got to bed.

As usual, Sully went completely overboard on his new hobby. He bought half a dozen sets of cars and had a special case built to carry them in. His racing cars kept the boys amused on the road all season.

One day, when I saw him at a football game in California, where he lived his first couple of years with the Red Sox, he told me he had gone into the fiber glass diving board business.

"I've got it made, Curt," he said. "I'm manufacturing these things with a couple of partners and we're swamped with orders. We'll make a mint."

The following spring I asked him at Sarasota, "How are you doing with your fiber glass diving boards?"

"It didn't work," he said. "But we've got a real good thing going instead. We chopped the boards into little pieces, and we're selling them as struts for airplanes."

"You chopped up the boards?"

"Yes, and it's going to be terrific. Imagine—a ten-ton support just from a little piece of fiber glass. It'll be the greatest thing that ever happened to aviation. We'll sell these things by the millions."

The next time I asked him about business he said, "We dissolved the corporation. Dropped the whole thing. But we didn't take much of a loss."

"What are you selling now?" I asked him. "Fiber glass toothpicks?"

"No," he said. "I'm going to buy a boat, sail it to Florida, and go into the real estate business there."

He did, too. He took a course in navigation, learned how to sail, and left right after the season ended.

Sully was terrific on the air. He loved to talk, and he did it well. One spring I asked him what kind of a season he thought he'd have.

"Curt," he replied, "I'm in the twilight of a mediocre career."

His closest pal was Sammy White, a rather strange character with ice blue eyes that bored right through you. The only thing that kept him from being a great catcher was his arm, which was only so-so. But he was a marvelous receiver, and he knew how to handle pitchers.

You never knew whether Sammy was riding you or not. He would walk up, stare at you with those glittering eyes, and say, "I'm a lousy catcher, ain't I?"

This gave you the Hobson's choice of agreeing and getting a punch in the nose or disagreeing and getting into an argument. Once, I tried to get out from under by saying, "You're a great catcher, Sammy. You're just not hitting."

It didn't work. White glared at me and snapped, "So I'm a lousy hitter, huh?" That started another argument.

He always carried a little tape recorder and a black notebook. He clammed up when I asked him about the recorder, but he told me the notebook was to keep track of opposing hitters. "It's the greatest book on hitters in baseball," he used to say. "It'll be worth a lot of money some day."

Sammy had been a basketball star at the University of Washington. One night Leo Egan, televising a Boston Celtics game locally, spotted White in the audience and got him to come down to the floor at halftime. They talked a few minutes, then Egan said, "Sam, you used to play basketball. Want to take a little shot?"

"I wouldn't mind," White answered. "I haven't touched a ball in a long time."

He took off his coat, stood at the foul line, and popped the ball in.

"That's pretty good," Egan said. "Want to try another?"

"Sure," Sammy said.

He backed up five feet and popped in another.

By this time the crowd was beginning to cheer, and I perked up at the television set at home. After he backed up another five or six feet and hit for the third time in a row, Sammy said, "That's enough for one day."

"Just one more," Egan coaxed.

Sammy shrugged, moved back a few more feet, and dropped a high, arching shot through the hoop. The crowd was roaring for more, so White said, "Oh, well, I might as well go all the way."

He moved back to midcourt, took careful aim, and fired. The ball went through for the fifth straight time, and everyone in the Garden went crazy. Then White picked up his coat, put it on, and said, "Thank you, ladies and gentlemen," and casually walked off the floor.

He didn't have any better luck in business than Sullivan did. He quit playing ball rather than leave Boston when the Red Sox traded him in the winter of 1960, and opened a big bowling alley. It still bears his name, but White no longer has an interest in it.

I lost track of both him and Sullivan for a couple of years. All I knew was that both were divorced and had left town.

In January of 1965 I went to Honolulu to broadcast the Hula Bowl football game. One day the phone rang, and it was Sully.

"What are you doing here?" I asked.

"Sammy and I are living on one of the other islands."

"Working?"

"We've got a great deal cooking," Sully said. "Curt, we'll make a fortune. I'll tell you about it some time."

I wonder what it was. Next time I'm in Hawaii maybe I'll find out.

Jackie Jensen was one of the finest athletes I've ever seen. He had fantastic muscular coordination, tremendous strength, great determination, and a physique that seemed indestructible. When he first came to the Yankees in 1949— the same year I did—he was a glamour boy with everything going for him. He had been an All-America back at the University of California, and had starred in the Rose Bowl and the East-West game. He was also such a good college baseball player that he had commanded a sizable bonus. A handsome youth with blue eyes and blond hair, he had just married the former Zoe Ann Olsen, a beautiful blonde Olympic diving star. They drove into the Yankees' training camp in a gold Cadillac convertible.

The Yankees couldn't have cared less about Jensen. The brass paid little attention to him and most of the players wouldn't give him the right time. They resented his looks, his background, and his bonus. He spent a miserable season sitting on the bench. Two years later, when I went to Boston, Jackie was just beginning to get into the Yankee lineup. But they weren't happy with him nor he with them, and they finally traded him to Washington.

I was having lunch at Fenway Park with Cronin and Yawkey one day when Joe suddenly got up to leave.

"Where are you going?" Yawkey said.

"I want to look at somebody," he said.

The Senators were in town, and I couldn't imagine anyone on that club who might interest Cronin. I joined him in back of the grandstand and asked.

"Jensen," Joe replied. "We need a right-handed power hitter. I think he'd be perfect for Fenway Park, and he'd do well on the road, too."

Not long after that, the Red Sox got Jensen for Maurice McDermott and Tom Umphlett. At the time, it looked like a steal for the Senators. McDermott had won eighteen games the year before and Umphlett had hit .283. Jensen, although showing occasional flashes, had never become a star. After he made the deal Cronin took such a roasting from the experts that I asked him if he was sorry.

"Wait," he said.

In the next six years Jensen led the American League in runs batted in three times and was once its Most Valuable Player. McDermott never had another good year and neither did Umphlett.

But Jackie had problems. Flying terrified him. He couldn't sleep for days before a flight, had to force himself into an airplane, literally sweated out every trip, and was a nervous wreck on arrival.

Jackie retired for a year. Then at Lake Tahoe where he lived he met a hypnotist who offered to help him. He made such good progress that he soon flew with the hypnotist with no ill effects, and it appeared that he had his trouble licked. He returned to the Red Sox the following spring, and was very optimistic—as long as the hypnotist was around. Until 1961 he had been able to make most hops by train, but then Los Angeles joined the league and air travel became mandatory.

But by the time the Red Sox broke camp in Scottsdale, Arizona, the hypnotist had gone. Jensen began brooding about the trip to Boston. The exhibition game schedule required almost daily flights, and Jackie couldn't face them. He went to Manager Mike Higgins and said, "I'll fly when

I have to during the regular season, but don't make me fly now."

Higgins announced Jackie had a groin injury and sent him to Boston for treatment. But the only treatment Jensen got was by a psychiatrist. Although the psychiatrist apparently didn't help him, Jackie felt fine when we arrived. His hypnotist from Lake Tahoe had come to town to appear in a Boston night club. He spent all his spare time with Jensen, who got special permission to let him come and go as he pleased in the Red Sox locker room.

Frank Malzone was suffering from torn tendons in his ankle after a sliding mishap in Scottsdale a month earlier. The injury took forever to heal, and Malzone was pretty discouraged. On the day before the season opened he was lying in the clubhouse under a heat lamp when Jensen brought this hypnotist in.

"Why don't you let him help you, Frank?" Jackie said. "He's helped me."

"I'll try anything," Malzone said. "My ankle isn't getting any better. I can't even put my weight on it. It hurts something terrible when I try to stand."

"I think I can help you if you'll cooperate," the hypnotist told him.

"I'll cooperate," Frank said. "I'm cooperating already."

While he lay on the trainer's table in his shorts and half a dozen of us stood around watching, the hypnotist quietly said, "Frank, think of a nice mountain lake with clear, cool, blue water." He stared at Malzone, took a watch on a chain out of his pocket, let it swing gently in front of Malzone's eyes, and murmured, "Clear mountain lake, Frank—clear blue lake—blue lake—beautiful and quiet—Frank—you're going to sleep now . . ." the watch was waving back and forth and there wasn't a sound in the room except for the soft voice of the hypnotist.

"Mountain lake—soft and beautiful and quiet . . ." the

voice was like velvet ". . . clear and blue—you're going to sleep, Frank—sleep—sleep—sleep . . ."

The watch kept waving, the hypnotist kept talking, and Malzone's eyes half-closed. Pretty soon the hypnotist said, "Now, Frank, I want you to get up off that table and walk around the room. You can do it all right. It won't hurt a bit. All the pain will be gone."

We stood, fascinated and mystified, while the hypnotist repeated the instructions in his soothing voice. After a while Malzone sat up and dangled his legs.

"Don't be afraid, Frank—put your foot down and walk. . . . It won't hurt—won't hurt . . ."

Malzone finally put his foot down.

"*Gawdalmighty*—" he shrieked.

He hopped back on the table, swearing and panting in anguish. The hypnotist turned away, disgusted. "Wouldn't cooperate," he muttered.

Apparently Jensen stopped cooperating, too, because flying began bothering him again even with his Svengali around. Once we had afternoon games on successive days at Fenway Park and in Detroit. As soon as the Boston game ended Jackie rushed out to his car, which the hypnotist had all warmed up for him, and the two drove like mad to Albany to catch the New England States, a train which had already left Boston while the game was still on. They had to average ninety miles an hour, but they made it. This, of course, was to avoid the danger of flying. Another time they drove all night right through to Detroit. Jensen, dog-tired and lucky to be alive after such a wild trip from Boston, arrived in time for the game, triumphant that he had ducked another plane ordeal.

He was too intelligent not to realize the absurdity of the situation. After half a season of going to all manner of ridiculous extremes to reach ball games on time without flying, Jackie jumped the club and went home to Lake Tahoe. He made one more attempt to keep going, joining us in Los Angeles after another course of instruction and encouragement from the hypnotist. Scared to death but game as ever, he flew east with us and played until he had another flight to face. Then he quit for good. I hated to see him go. He was a nice guy and a fine ballplayer. Too bad he had that complex.

Gene Conley was one of my favorites. He came to the Red Sox from the Phillies in an even swap for Frank Sullivan—a true character-for-character deal. Conley, an amiable giant who stood six feet eight inches, was also a full-time professional basketball player, starring for the Boston Celtics as backup man for Bill Russell. How he did it is beyond me, for he was under pressure twelve months of the year, but he lasted several seasons as the only major league two-sport athlete of his time.

Conley was an alpine Ellis Kinder, a great competitor on the field, but good-natured, easy-going, gentle, and relaxed off it. Despite his endurance, the big guy lacked Kinder's recuperative powers. If he saw a long night ahead, he knew he couldn't pitch the next day, so he alerted manager Mike Higgins.

"I don't know how late I'll stay out tonight," he would say. "I may not be around tomorrow."

He was such a good guy and he worked so hard that Higgins let him do pretty much as he pleased. Something of a loner, Conley rarely took other ballplayers on his rounds, so, with one exception, his activities never affected anyone else. The exception was Pumpsie Green, the first Negro to play for the Red Sox. He and Conley became buddies.

Pumpsie would go anywhere Gene would go until one evening in 1962 when the two were involved in a hilarious escapade. It started on a bus from Yankee Stadium to the Newark airport. Traffic was heavy, the late afternoon sun was beating down, and it was murderously hot.

"Wouldn't a nice cold beer go good right about now,

Pumps?" Conley remarked when the bus got stuck on a bridge in a traffic jam.

"It sure would, Geno," Green agreed.

"This bus isn't going anywhere for a while," said Conley. "Let's get off. We've got plenty of time."

The two got off the bus and took a taxi back into New York. They wandered all over town, stopping for a little refreshment whenever the spirit moved them. In the meantime, the Red Sox bus finally got going again, and the team flew to Washington without them.

Both Conley and Green later told me what happened. As the long evening wore on Conley had a brilliant idea.

"Pumps," he said, "let's go to Israel."

"Israel?"

"Yeah. We'll go to Israel and rent one of those two-humped camels. You ride in front and I'll ride in back. We'll get a couple of six-packs of beer, and we can drink it out in the desert."

"Who needs Israel?" Green said. "I've got troubles enough in this country."

"If you don't go to Israel with me I'll drink your six-pack while I'm out on that camel," Conley threatened.

"Go ahead. But I'm going to Washington."

"Look, Pumps, they need us in Israel. They're just starting sports there and we can help them."

They argued while Conley went to the Commodore Hotel, where the Red Sox stayed in New York, to cash a check for a thousand dollars. After he had the money he said, "Sure you don't want to go, Pumps? I've got enough for both our fares."

But Green, who had always gone everywhere with Conley, drew the line at Israel. Conley, with you-let-me-down-in-the-clutch sadness, said goodbye and got into a taxi. It was after midnight, the story had broken that the boys had missed connections to Washington, and the cab driver was a baseball fan.

"Aren't you Gene Conley?" he asked.

"That's right."

"The Red Sox have been looking all over for you guys."

"They'll see Pumpsie pretty soon but not me," Conley said. "I'm going to Israel."

He would have, too, but they wouldn't let him on the plane because he didn't have a passport.

Just when I thought the Red Sox were running out of characters, along came Dick Stuart. He had the biggest ego in baseball, but was such a friendly guy you couldn't dislike him. He talked constantly about himself—his strength, his batting prowess, his looks, his clothes, his ability to do anything better than anyone else. He had the most powerful wrists I ever saw. One of his many sources of pride was his proficiency as an Indian wrestler. With good reason he called himself baseball's uncrowned Indian wrestling king. Although often challenged, he never lost a match while with the Red Sox.

We got Stu in a winter trade with the Pirates in 1963. A powerful right-handed-hitting first baseman, he was probably the world's worst fielder. He could handle thrown balls and line drives, but everything else was a mystery to him. When "Stonefingers" or "Dr. Strangeglove," as they called him, was faced with a ground ball or a pop fly, anything might happen.

He was at his worst on grounders hit right at him—he'd fumble them or kick them or let them go between his legs. He probably turned more routine outs into triples than any first baseman in history. He ran pitchers ragged because, no matter where he fielded a grounder hit in his direction, the pitcher had to come over to cover first. Stu was a menace on pop-ups. The safest thing to do was get out of his way. He once nearly broke Earl Wilson's ribs when they collided going after one. Stu was always yelling for somebody else to take it, then dashing madly after it himself at the last minute.

Low automobile license plates are a status symbol in Massachusetts. One day Dick Radatz said to Stu, "They ought to give you E-3. Then everyone would know who you were."

Tony Oliva of the Twins lost his bat missing a swing one night. It flew toward first base, then rolled very slowly. While it was still barely moving, Stu reached for it and missed. When he finally grabbed it, the fans gave him a big cheer.

"That's the first time I ever saw a guy get a hand for fielding a bat," Radatz remarked later.

"You should have seen them in Pittsburgh when I picked up a gum wrapper one night," Stu replied. "They gave me a standing ovation."

During his first year in Boston he conducted a television sports show that was the answer to an egocentric's dream. I started watching it once, when Carl Yastrzemski was his guest.

"Hi, there," Stu began. "I'm Dick Stuart and welcome to the Dick Stuart Show. The guest on the Dick Stuart Show tonight is Carl Yastrzemski of the Red Sox. It's great to have you on the Dick Stuart Show, Carl."

"It's great to be on the Dick Stuart Show," Yastrzemski said.

"Yes, sir, it's nice to have you on the Dick Stuart Show," Stu said. "You've never been on the Dick Stuart Show before, have you, Carl?"

That was about as much as I could take. I turned it off.

Tall, handsome, blue-eyed and black-haired, Stu's extensive wardrobe was one of his proudest possessions. He always took four or five suits on every road trip, and was so fussy about the creases in his trousers that he carried a garment bag for them. The bulky bag was a nuisance everywhere, especially on airplanes and on buses to and from airports. Stewardesses had to look for extra space, and bus drivers for special places. Baggage compartments were out. Stu wouldn't think of risking his precious creases there.

Most buses have metal poles running on both sides from front to back for standees to hang on to. Stu used them for his garment bag. He talked so much about how sharp his clothes looked when traveling that a couple of other ball-players also got garment bags for their suits and slacks. By 1964, Stu's second year on the club, practically every-one had them. This not only drove stewardesses nuts but scared the daylights out of bus drivers. Every time a bus made a turn the garment bags slid along the poles with a clatter that sounded as if we were hit by a truck. Naturally, there were squawks, but nobody did anything about it ex-cept poll the ballplayers. Since most of them carried garment bags by then, they voted to keep them.

Just before the season ended Billy Herman became the Red Sox manager. "Starting next year," he said, "no more garment bags."

I've often wondered what Stu would have done about that. The question never came up because the Red Sox traded him to the Phillies during the winter. Without him to champion the cause of garment bags the other ball-players let it die. In 1965 they went back to suitcases.

13

Although I have always preferred announcing baseball, football, and basketball because these are the spectator sports that interest the most people and capture the largest audiences, I enjoy occasional off-beat assignments. Just before the Argentine fishing trip in 1962, I had one in Germany for A.B.C. It was our report for "Wide World of Sports" of the world bobsled racing championships at Garmisch-Partenkirchen.

Garmisch, a lovely Bavarian village sixty miles from Munich, was the site of Hitler's 1936 Winter Olympics. Because of this association, I went over there prepared to dislike both the place and its people. It was impossible to dislike the place, for its gorgeous Alpine setting in midwinter is breathtakingly beautiful. Some of the people looked and acted like unreconstructed Nazis, but the vast majority were warmly cooperative and anxious to please. For me, the trip served as a preliminary for my coverage two years later of the 1964 Winter Olympics.

Before going to Garmisch I knew no more about bobsled racing than curling. I had never seen a bobsled, let alone a race, and had never met a bobsled racer. I went with Roone Arledge and an A.B.C. director from Chicago, Jim Holmes. We had a marvelously efficient German crew from Intertel, one of Europe's most successful television producing companies. The expert who worked with me was Stan Benham, the United States bobsled coach and a former star in this highly dangerous sport.

Benham was already in Garmisch when we arrived. I pictured him as a wiry, dashing character full of fire and bounce, with a ramrod back and piercing eyes. Somebody called to tell me he was on his way, and a few minutes later a dumpy little guy with thick glasses slouched into my hotel room.

"Curt Gowdy?" he asked, taking his hand out of his jacket pocket long enough to offer it to me.

"That's right," I said.

"I'm Stan Benham."

What he lacked in looks Benham made up for in knowledge and—as other bobsled people told me later—guts. In his racing days he had been an utterly fearless driver who knew how to take advantage of every opportunity. The sport requires split-second reflexes, particularly on the driver, who must make life-or-death decisions faster than most people can think.

Bobsledders are probably the most exclusive group of athletes in existence. They have to be, for there are less than half a dozen places in the whole world where they can practice or compete. Lake Placid, New York has the only bobsled run in the Western Hemisphere. The others are in Europe, one at Garmisch, one in Italy, one at St. Moritz, and one built especially for the 1964 Olympics at Innsbruck, Austria.

Since the courses must have concrete or stone foundations and be constructed according to precise dimensions to keep the safety factor within reason, they are tremendously expensive to build. Naturally, a cold climate, where the thermometer gets down below freezing for sustained periods of time, is essential. And, since the courses must be downhill, the best places for them are in mountainous areas.

Garmisch is a perfect setting, a high-altitude village on the shores of a lake which freezes early enough in the fall so that by winter ice can be taken from it in blocks. The bobsled run there is made of ice, packed perfectly on top of a stone base. The run has different types of curves, each of which presents a separate problem, much as the holes of a golf course present a variety of problems to the people who play it.

The trick in bobsledding is to try to stay in the middle of the course, bouncing off the sides as little as possible. Every slip, every bump, every change of direction, every inch off the middle costs fractions of seconds which mean the difference between victory and defeat. Losses by a twentieth of a second are common in bobsled racing. The team a half second off the winner's time can finish down among the also-rans.

Teams are usually made up of four men, although they also have two-man races. The start and the curves are the most vital parts of the race. In four-man events, the driver sits in front. The second and third men are there for balance and ballast. They function much as the middle oarsmen of a crew. They must know their business, which way to lean and how to react to the drivers' moves, but they are soldiers, not officers.

The brake man sits in the rear, and, while he uses his judgment on the way down, his greatest importance is his ability to get the sled off to a fast start. The four men rock the sled back and forth three times at the start. They thrust forward at the count of three, then jump on, the driver getting aboard first, followed by the second and third men. The brake man must give an already fast-moving vehicle one final thrust before jumping on himself. If he does the job properly he can save as much as a full second. Sometimes he misses the sled altogether, which automatically means disqualification. When this happens, the driver steers the sled the length of the course without a brake man, a pretty tricky job in itself.

Once the team gets off to a good start, everything is up to the driver. Having had many practice runs, he knows where and what type the curves are and how best to take them. He rides them much like an auto race driver, going as tightly as he dares, to save those precious fractional seconds.

At ninety miles an hour a wrong guess could result in disaster. If he takes the banks too high he risks flying off the course. If he sticks too closely to the middle he risks turning over.

Stan Benham led me to a shed where the sleds were kept between runs. We found everyone honing runners, a chore that consumes far more of a bobsled racer's time than racing. The runners are rounded, like regular sled runners, and so precisely shaved that the width and the rate of the curve must be measured with calipers. These dimensions are prescribed by regulations.

Stan introduced me around. Practically all of the racers spoke English, so I had no trouble communicating with them. Most were working people, but several were sportsmen of substantial means. Inside that shed and on the bobsled run you couldn't tell one from the other.

The Italians, led by Eugenio Monti, were the world's champions. Monti, a short red-headed man in his thirties, who ran a popular ski area in Italy, was terribly scarred from winter sports accidents. A former ski champion, he had suffered multiple injuries in a bad spill. When he recovered he turned to the far more dangerous sport of bobsled racing. In the years that followed he acquired eight world's championships, innumerable scars, and a new nose. His own was smashed in a racing mishap.

Benham told me that Monti was the most patient and careful bobsled driver in the world. Each morning he went to the top of the course and walked down, marking certain turns with twigs which he took off trees and stuck in snowbanks. Again I thought in terms of golf. Monti read a course the way a golfer reads a putting green. By race time, he knew every square inch of it. A friendly little guy who was always willing to help other racers, he was extremely popular among them.

The Canadian bobsledders were a wild group of characters who played as hard as they worked. Two were from the bush region of northern Canada, and all were hard-fighting, hard-drinking, devil-may-care men whose favorite pastimes were racing and enjoying life.

The Americans were nice young fellows, most of whom came from Lake Placid. Not many Americans anywhere else are interested in bobsled racing. The trouble is most championships are held abroad on courses Europeans know well from having practiced on them so often.

One of the sport's most colorful figures is Tony Nash, millionaire English manufacturer who keeps his country in bobsledding by financing periodic team trips to St. Moritz for practice. Outgoing and energetic, with a bubbling personality and a huge smile, he looks no more like an adventurous sportsman than Benham. He is a short, balding bachelor in his forties, who gives the appearance of a stodgy young British clubman, but dispels that as soon as he opens his mouth, for he is a fascinating talker.

Nash told me he first went down a bobsled course at Garmisch on a dare while in the British Army during World War II. He was hooked after one run.

"The attraction of bobsledding," he said, "comes from many factors—the speed, the danger, the glaring ice, the fine nuances of driving and hitting curves and coming out of them just right, the roar, the flash, the wind going by you. It's impossible to describe."

Nash's brake man at Garmisch was the dashing Captain the Honorable T. Robin Dixon of Her Majesty's Grenadier Guards.

By his own admission, Dixon could never be called a spendthrift. The bobsledders use little wire holders in the toes of their boots for traction on the pushoffs.

"I buy mine by the dozen," he told me. "I get a penny off that way."

We had to wait two days for the races because the weather was unseasonably warm. On the third day it was snowing hard with the thermometer ten above zero, and the races were on. I went over to the course with the rest of our crew, arriving at about eight in the morning. Benham and I worked at the finish line. We could see only the very end of the race, but we watched the rest of it on a monitor. The sleds traveled so fast there was no other way to cover them. Eight television cameras and strategically placed microphones gave us the sights and sounds of the whole course.

The day began with practice runs. The first one didn't impress me at all. When the sled hit the curves it hardly seemed to be moving.

"There's nothing to it," I told Benham. "That one didn't go very fast."

"It didn't, eh?" he said. "Come on over to the last curve."

We walked up the hill to the final curve on the course and waited for the next practice run. I watched the monitor there as the sled shoved off, and I saw it passing the first curve, and still wasn't impressed. It went by the second curve and the one after that before I realized my mistake. Up at the curve we could hear much better, and the roar of the approaching bobsled was louder and louder. Suddenly, there came a "va-room!" and a black streak whistled by so fast that I stepped back instinctively.

Benham was grinning when I turned to him and said, "I see what you mean."

The slow-motion effect was caused by the cameras. They caught the sleds from a frontal, rather than a lateral, angle, which minimized the speed.

The championships, won by the Italians, went on all day. By that time, having stood in the snow in ten-degree temperature for more than nine hours, I was just about congealed. Yet, cold as I was, I got a tremendous kick out of the day's events. I left Garmisch in hopes that I hadn't seen the last of the tightly knit little group of madcap men who make up the world's complement of bobsled racers.

I hadn't. Two years later I was on the A.B.C. crew that

televised the winter Olympics at Innsbruck. I got the bobsled racing assignment because I had covered the 1962
championships. Besides four-man and two-man team races,
the Olympic Games had added a new event called the
luge. This is a singles race on a hand sled controlled by
movements of the body and legs. It is one of the world's
oldest sports, originating with the Romans, whose legions
used the luge to get around the Alps.

The luge course at Innsbruck was a miniature bobsled
course, with narrow lanes and serpentine turns. It turned
out to be even more dangerous than the bobsled run. When
three contestants were killed flying off curves and banging
into trees in practice runs, the rest refused to go down
until the committee built high boards at the curves. There
were some bad accidents even after that was done, but no
one else was killed.

At the start, the luge racer sits on his sled with his feet
on the steering bar in front. As he starts down the run he
lies flat on his back, causing less wind resistance and creating more speed. Every so often he must raise his head a
trifle to peer between his feet and see where he's going,
but only for a split second. Mad as bobsledding is, the
luge is madder. I think it's the most dangerous sport I ever
saw. There was an American team made up of soldiers
stationed in Europe. They were overmatched and finished
last.

"We didn't expect to do any better," one told me. "We
went into this thing for fun, and we had plenty. It's a
great sport, but just for over here. There aren't any courses
in the States and I doubt if any will ever be built."

Tony Nash and Captain Dixon pulled a big upset by
beating the Italians for the two-man championship, and I
never saw two happier men.

"Ever since that day I first went down a run I've wanted
to win the Olympics," Nash yelled. "Now I've done it."

"Has England ever won a gold medal in the winter games?" I asked him.

"Never. And that makes the victory even sweeter."

"What are you going to do now, Tony?"

"I'm going over to lunch, old chap," he said. "And it's going to be the most liquid lunch anyone ever had."

Just before the four-man finals, I asked Monti if he expected to win.

"I doubt it," he said. "I don't know what's wrong, but I can't seem to get going. I'm driving very poorly."

I asked Benham, Nash, and one or two others what they thought of the Italian's chances. Nash expressed everyone's opinion when he said, "The course is too easy for a great driver like Monti. The tougher it is, the greater the problem and the more Monti works at it. He can't get going because the course doesn't challenge him."

Tony was right. Monti and his Italian team were beaten in another upset, this time by the Canadians.

I broadcast some hockey and speed skating, two sports about which I knew very little. I practiced for the hockey by going to Bruins' games in Boston with Bill Liston, an able Boston *Traveler* sportswriter and a former schoolboy hockey player. I took a tape recorder with me, sat in the press box with Bill and did some dry runs, playing the tapes back later to see how I sounded. Bill listened to my tapes and told me what I did wrong. So did the late Walter Brown. Although Brown was one of the world's best-known professional promoters—he was president of the Boston Garden and of the Bruins, and owner of the fabulous Boston Celtics—his first and dearest love was amateur hockey. He helped start the Winter Olympics and wouldn't think of missing one. Jerre and I spent many pleasant hours with him and his wife at Innsbruck.

One of our toughest jobs over there was digging up background dope on hockey players from other countries. The Russians had the best team, but they wouldn't talk. I didn't see them even show any emotion until the very end. After they beat Canada in the finals they banged their sticks on the ice and threw their arms around each other. They looked happy until outsiders approached, then they clammed up. I couldn't get near them.

The first game I covered was between the United States and Rumania. I wouldn't have found out much about those fellows either except for Stan Benham. He knew the Rumanian bobsledders, and through them got me a date at the Olympic Village with the coach and the captain of their hockey team.

All smiles—thanks to Benham—they met me in the front office and took me to their quarters. They didn't speak much English, but grins, gestures, and a bottle of Rumanian brandy filled that gap very nicely. A couple of the players were already working on the brandy when we arrived. The minute I walked in they poured me a drink.

I had one sip and nearly jumped out the window. The stuff tasted like gasoline and went down like fire. It took a bit of getting used to, but I ended up having a fine time while learning a good deal about the Rumanian hockey team.

They had no roster, so I took a piece of paper and wrote down numbers. When I came to one worn by somebody on the team, they all grinned, sang out his name in chorus, and somebody spelled it out for me. The coach knew a few English words, and he understood that I wanted to know what these boys did for a living. That led us into a game of charades.

One player was a carpenter. When I asked about him, the boys pretended they were beating the air with a hammer. Another was an electrician. They showed me this by unscrewing a light bulb. Most of the players were students, indicated by picking up a book and pretending to read it.

I asked if the team was any good and the coach shook his head while repeating, "No, no." When I asked about the Russians, he nodded and said, "Yes—yes—" I asked why, and he pulled out his wallet, fingering the money in it.

"Professionals?" I said.

He nodded. The others suddenly went silent.

"Do you like them?" I asked the coach.

He pointed to the wall with one hand and touched an ear with the other, telling me that walls have ears.

"You mean, 'no comment'?" I said.

He nodded again, and smiled. When the others saw that, they smiled, too, and we dropped the subject.

Somebody brought in a little doll dressed in Rumanian costume and gave it to me. Somebody else gave me an ashtray. Before I left, we swapped pins, a popular pastime at the Olympics. I had an A.B.C. pin with a camera etched on it which I handed the coach in exchange for his Rumanian team pin.

Through Benham I met coaches and members of several other European hockey teams. They were friendly and helpful, and I liked them, but none equaled the Rumanians in fun and hospitality.

The speed skating star of the Olympics was Lydia Skoblikova of Russia, who won four gold medals. A big, powerful blonde with a ruddy complexion, she seemed friendly enough but couldn't speak a word of English. At press conferences she always smiled and answered questions quickly through an interpreter. Then, somebody in her party would curtly say, "That's all," and that *was* all. I got the impression she was enjoying herself and would like to have stayed longer.

The only Russian athlete I got anywhere with was Oleg Protopopov who, with his wife, Ludmilla Belousova, upset Marika Kilius and Hans-Jurgen Baumler of West Germany to win the figure skating pairs title. Protopopov had learned to speak very good English in only two years, and was eager to demonstrate. I asked him if he considered his victory over the German favorites an upset.

"Oh, no," he said. "I am like anyone going to a war. I came here to be a general, not a corporal. We came here to win, and we did."

"Your music was magnificent," I said. "How did you select it?"

"It is Russian," he replied. "Where could we find better music than our own Rachmaninoff?"

The United States picked up an unexpected gold medal when Terry McDermott, a twenty-three-year-old barber from Essexville, Michigan, won the 500-meter speed skating championship. Olympic—and European—speed skaters always race against the clock, two competitors at a time. McDermott was paired with Evgeni Grishin, a Russian who had won two previous Olympic gold medals. Terry got off to a tremendous start and whipped over the course a full half second ahead of the Russian. Nobody else came much closer and McDermott won easily.

I had one quick interview with McDermott, who, because of his extreme shyness, was rather uncommunicative. A sort of "Aw, shucks" youth, he didn't seem to realize the extent of his tremendous upset victory. I would like to have spent more time with him, but I was tied up with bobsled races, which were just beginning.

Our whole crew was always tied up with something. Every day was like covering two or three "Wide World of Sports" shows at once. Jim McKay, Jim Simpson, and I did the announcing, assisted by specialists in each sport. The technical details were handled by separate and complete television crews, each covering some event in detail. The whole business then was funneled through Doug Wilson and Ron Hawkins, the assistant directors. They had the toughest job of all, for besides attending the events they had to go through thousands of feet of video tape to edit them down to usable length on the air. There was one stretch of three days and nights when Wilson and Hawkins had no sleep at all, and I doubt if they averaged two hours a night the whole time they were there.

Every precaution was taken to allow for slipups or emergencies. Our best hope was to put the show on the air by satellite, but this wasn't always possible. The alternative was to rush a set of pictures to Munich every morning to meet a five o'clock Lufthansa flight due in New York around noon. The films were driven from Innsbruck by Colonel Jim McNew, who volunteered his services. Thanks to remarkably good weather, McNew never missed the flight.

But we had to be prepared for the chance that he might. We knew the New York schedules of every flight from cities within several hundred miles of Innsbruck. If necessary, we would have chartered a plane out of Munich to make one of them. Even in New York, A.B.C. took no chances. In case driving conditions to the city were impossible, the network had emergency telecasting equipment at Kennedy Airport, with a full operating crew standing by.

On arrival at Kennedy, the films were taken downtown to A.B.C. where they were re-edited before going on the air. Sometimes something went wrong with the sound, or voices and pictures weren't properly synchronized, or somebody would have pulled a boner everyone in Innsbruck had overlooked. Nothing could be done when we telecast by satellite because that was live, but when we didn't, corrections were necessary. For this purpose alone, we were all on call twenty-four hours a day.

It was a wildly wonderful three weeks. We worked hard, slept little, ate at crazy hours, and were always tired, but I wouldn't swap the experience for anything.

I'd go through it again any time, and I could never get too much of it. After all, it happens only once every four years.

14

They say there's nothing new in football, and after what happened to me I'm willing to believe it. In 1951 in a game between Boston University and Villanova I saw an incident so unusual that I would have bet everything I owned it would never be repeated.

B.U. was closing out a disappointing season on a rainy day in Philadelphia. Villanova got rolling early, and pretty soon had a big lead. Late in the game it became foggy and hard to see, so I wasn't sure what was going on. A Villanova back broke away, apparently headed for a touchdown, but he suddenly went down. I couldn't understand why, because he had outrun the whole B.U. team.

I was even more mystified when Villanova lined up on the B.U. two-yard line to try for a point after touchdown. I turned to Joe Costanza, who worked as a spotter and statistician with me that year, and asked him if he knew what happened.

"You've got me, Curt," he said. "New rules, I guess."

After the game we went to the B.U. dressing room to ask Coach Buff Donelli for the answer.

"It was an automatic touchdown for Villanova," Buff said.

"An automatic touchdown?"

"That's right. Mario Mauriello came off our bench and tackled the Villanova runner."

"I never saw anything like that before," I commented.

"No," Donelli said, "and you probably never will again."

Two years later I did the Cotton Bowl game between Rice and Alabama in Dallas. Dickie Moegle, Rice's All-

America back, was having a tremendous day. In the third quarter, with Rice apparently pinned down back around its fifteen-yard-line, Moegle suddenly broke loose, and by the time he reached the forty-yard-line there wasn't anybody near him except a couple of his own teammates. Unless he tripped and fell flat on his face, he was headed for the longest touchdown run of the ball game.

Suddenly Red Lewis jumped off the Alabama bench, ran out to the field, and brought Moegle down. Everyone in the Cotton Bowl, including Lewis, was stunned. As soon as I realized what happened, I said, "That'll be an automatic touchdown." Sure enough, the referee gave one to Rice.

"How did you know?" somebody asked me.

"I saw it happen before," I said.

I'll bet I'm the only announcer who ever did.

One of the most peculiar games I ever covered was between Miami and Pittsburgh in 1961. That was the first appearance in varsity competition for George Mira of Miami, perhaps the best college passer of recent years. On the day before the game Paul Christman and I watched him in action. He threw a hard, sizzling pass, squarely on the target.

"Should I try to slow him up?" Coach Andy Gustafson asked Paul.

"Don't touch him," Christman said. "He's a fine natural passer. Sure, he fires the ball hard, but your receivers will have to get used to him. He's one of the best young passers I've seen in years."

The next day the game began in perfect weather. The temperature was around seventy-five or eighty, the sun was shining, there wasn't a cloud in the sky, and a big crowd in Miami's Orange Bowl settled back to watch the debut of a great new star. Mira didn't disappoint anyone. He had speed and poise, ran the club like a veteran, and his bullet passes were tough to knock down and almost impossible to intercept. Although Pitt had a fine team, Mira dominated the play in the first half, during which he passed Miami to a touchdown.

Halfway through the second period huge black clouds began rolling in from the ocean. Paul and I both mentioned on the air that we might have a squall, which we hoped wouldn't hit until the end of the half and would be over by the time the second half began.

Squall? It was one of the most violent storms I can remember. It began just before the half ended, and when the gun sounded the rain was coming down in solid sheets while the wind whistled up to fifty miles an hour. I never saw such a torrential rain last so long. The water kept pouring down until the field was a quagmire, the radio booth a bathtub, and the big crowd a sodden mass of drenched humanity.

It was still coming down when the second half began. With the field a mass of pools and slop, and the ball about as easy to grip as a greased pig, Mira was through passing for the day. Nobody could do much of anything, for the footing was as treacherous as the ball-handling. Pitt finally won on an eighty-yard run by Paul Martha after a double handoff during which everyone involved miraculously hung on to the ball. As he ran for his touchdown Martha threw back sheets of water like a truck ploughing through a puddle, but he stayed on his feet.

The two halves were like two different ball games, one played under the best possible conditions, the other under the worst. I've often wondered what would have happened if the weather hadn't changed so drastically. I doubt if anything short of a cloudburst could have stopped Mira.

Fog stopped everyone in the 1962 Grey Cup game between the Winnipeg Blue Bombers and the Hamilton Tiger-Cats at Toronto. Paul and I met Roone Arledge, Jim McKay, and the rest of the A.B.C. crew on the night before the game. The fog was so thick then that I don't know how we got into the airport, but the weather man promised it would clear up the next day.

It didn't. When we arrived at the stadium at eleven in the morning it looked as if we were in a cotton field. The visibility was so bad that Christman said, "Stick close, Curt, or we'll lose each other."

We walked along the field, and could barely see the yard lines there. When we got up to the television booth we couldn't even see where we had been.

An hour before the game the fog lifted enough so that we could see patches of the field. We talked back and forth with Roone, in the truck, and McKay, on the field, trying to dope out how to handle the situation.

"I can't see much up here, Roone," I said.

"Maybe it'll lift."

"What if it doesn't?"

"We'll have to kick things around somehow," he said. "Let's play it by ear."

Just before the game began the fog let up a little, giving Paul and me a pretty good view of the entire field. We went to work from the kickoff, and everything was fine until about halfway through the first period. Suddenly the fog came back, and there wasn't anything in front of us but a white window shade. I stumbled around on the air, then Roone told us, "McKay's down on the field and can see what's going on."

I switched to Jim just as somebody threw a touchdown pass, which he called perfectly. The fog was then down to about eight or ten feet, where it hovered over the field. We had one camera that could peek under it, so Jim and that camera did everything for the next few minutes. Then the fog rose and we picked up the broadcast again.

We did pretty well as the game progressed, only we were lost whenever there was a punt or a high pass. I'd give the passer's name, then say, "Now we switch to Jim McKay," and he'd say, "The pass was caught by so-and-so." There

were a flock of completions that day, but I didn't see more
than half a dozen.

The fog continued to hover over the field, never going
very far or very high. The people in the lower sections of
the stands and on the field were the only ones who saw
practically everything, but as the game went into the final
period even they were shut off. The fog suddenly clamped
down, socking the whole field in, and, as I turned the mike
over to McKay, there was a whistle to stop the game.

"Ladies and gentlemen," Jim said, "the Comissioner of
the Canadian Football League has just walked on the
field."

On our monitor was an incredible sight. The commissioner and the referee were walking together, but all we
could see were their heads and shoulders. The two floated
along like angels in the backfield.

"With wings and a lyre," somebody said, "they'd have
it made."

They talked a few minutes, then decided to postpone
the rest of the game until the next day. As they were
wafted off into space I signed off with, "We're sorry you
can't see the finish, but neither can we. A.B.C. will give you
a recap when it's over."

We had to leave that night for an A.F.L. game the next
afternoon, so we missed the last nine minutes of the only
championship football game that took twenty-four hours to
play. Hamilton won it in crisp, sunny, cloudless surroundings. The fog followed us out of town.

Three weeks later we ran into another strange finish. This
time it was the first six-quarter game in football history,
featuring, of all things, the toss of a coin.

The Houston Oilers and Dallas Texans were meeting in
Houston's Jepperson Stadium for the championship of the
then new and struggling American Football League. A sellout crowd of thirty-eight thousand came out for the game,
while millions more watched on national television.

Dallas led, 17–0, at the end of the first half, thanks to a superb passing exhibition by Len Dawson. George Blanda, Houston's quarterback, did just as fine a job in the second half, when the Oilers also scored two touchdowns and kicked a field goal. This tied the game at 17–17, sending it into overtime.

The officials and captains met at the fifty-yard-line for the coin toss to decide who would kick off and who would receive. Paul Christman and I switched from our mike in the booth to the shotgun mike on the field and put on our earphones to hear what was going on down there.

Dallas won the toss. To our amazement and, I'm sure, the amazement of everyone else, the Texans' captain, Abner Haynes, said, "We'll kick off to the scoreboard."

This meant that Dallas not only gave up the football but would kick against the wind to open a period in which the first team to score would win the game. Later, Coach Hank Stram of Dallas said he told Haynes to kick off if he won the toss, but only with the wind at his back. Haynes misunderstood his instructions.

As it turned out, Haynes' lapse wasn't as costly as it might have been because Houston failed to take advantage of the ball and the wind. The teams battled through a scoreless ten-minute fifth period, then moved into a sixth.

They changed sides, so Dallas finally faced in the right direction. Halfway through the period Bill Hull intercepted a Blanda pass to get the Texans off and running. They reached deep into Houston territory, and finally won a twenty-five-yard field goal by Tommy Brooker.

It was the longest pro football game in history, lasting seventy-seven minutes, fifty-four seconds, and fans still talk about it. I think that game was the turning point for the American League. Up to then, National League followers had looked down their noses at it. But from that time on, the A.F.L. was recognized for what it is—a bona fide major football league.

In December of 1964 Christman and I did football's first indoor bowl game, between Utah and West Virginia at Convention Hall in Atlantic City. It was a bitterly cold day, and we would have frozen outdoors. The promoters had brought in four inches of Merion blue grass turf which felt like wall-to-wall carpeting as you walked across it. The two coaches, Ray Nagel of Utah and Gene Corum of West Virginia, were delighted with the conditions. I don't know how happy Corum was after the game ended, for his club took a 32–6 beating, but at least he didn't risk pneumonia. Neither did we. It was a pleasure to watch a December game up North in civilized comfort.

Contrast this with the next day when we covered the eastern division A.F.L. finals between the Buffalo Bills and the Boston Patriots at Fenway Park. I had looked forward to doing a football game in my own back yard for a change, and I just hoped the weather wouldn't be impossible.

It was.

I woke up to a snowstorm. About an inch had been predicted, but one look out the window was all I needed to know this was no one-inch flurry. There were warnings on the radio for motorists to stay off the streets, and I would have been delighted to comply. It took me nearly an hour to get to the ball park, where I arrived about noon.

The snow kept piling up but the playing surface was covered with hay—170 tons of it—to keep the field from freezing over. The original plan was to remove the hay after an inch of snow had fallen, but when the snow didn't stop they decided to wait until the last minute. Just after I arrived, bulldozers and plows and tractors began pushing and hauling and scraping, treating the growing crowd to an unexpected bonus spectacle. Fenway Park holds about thirty-eight thousand for a football game, but the Patriots could have sold eighty thousand tickets. The weather and the traffic warnings didn't scare anybody away. New Englanders are hardy souls who would never let a little blizzard keep them from watching a football game, and they filled the ball park.

We had to kill half an hour while the field was being cleared. I used up the first part of it describing the scene and explaining the delay, while the cameras shifted around the field. Plows were scraping, bulldozers were piling up snow, tractors and jeeps were all over the place, and fans were running out to the field for hay to keep their feet warm. I shivered in the booth and Paul shivered on the field, where he interviewed the coaches, the quarterbacks, and any other players he could corral before coming up to join me. In the meantime, with all the markers out of sight, I lined up yard lines by landmarks—using boxes, rolled-up tarpaulins, tables, the ends of benches, anything that would serve as a guide.

When the field was cleared and the National Anthem was played, everything stopped. The fans took off their hats, the players their helmets, the workmen their caps. Bulldozer, tractor, and jeep drivers turned off their motors and snow removal crews lifted their plows. Everything stood at attention, even the mechanized equipment. As the last notes faded away, they all got moving again.

It was still snowing when the game began, and it kept on snowing for about the first quarter. When it stopped, the temperature, already below freezing, dropped even more. By halftime there wasn't a quiet set of teeth in the place. We might as well have been playing at the North Pole.

Since the kickoff was half an hour late, darkness fell long before the final gun sounded. Practically the entire last half was played under lights. Buffalo won the ball game, so the fans didn't even have the memory of a home team victory to keep them warm on the way home.

The only memory I had was of that nice comfortable Convention Hall in Atlantic City.

Up North, indoors is the only place to play football in midwinter.

15

Today the accent is on comfort and accessibility, and that includes sportscasters. We never had it so good. When we walk into a ball park or arena or stadium, the red carpet is out. Most professional sports organizations have what are popularly known in the trade as work and recreation rooms. There, representatives of all communications media and guests can eat, drink, and relax in air-conditioned or heated comfort, depending upon the climate.

Radio and working booths have been tremendously improved in recent years. We get the best seats in the house, with plenty of room to move around and, in some places, even swivel chairs with reclining seats. Statistics, notes, filler material, and personality sketches are right at hand. In some ball parks, attendants bring coffee or cold drinks during games, then gather luggage and have cabs ready when it's time to leave.

This is a far cry from the early days of broadcasting when announcers were scorned by the press and ignored by everyone else except the listening public. The first attempt at broadcasting was way back in 1912 when a couple of pioneers tried to do a University of Minnesota football game with a spark transmitter and regular telegraph signals. There was no indication that it ever went on the air, for no one could be found who heard it.

Station KDKA of Pittsburgh, the nation's first commercial radio station, did the first sports broadcast, a fight between Johnny Ray and Johnny Dundee at Pittsburgh's Motor Square Garden in April of 1921. The broadcast drew national publicity but not much else. Only a few hundred heard it.

The following July, David Sarnoff, then general manager of the Radio Corporation of America, created a radio station in Jersey City for the sole purpose of broadcasting the Jack Dempsey-Georges Carpentier world's heavyweight championship fight at Boyle's Thirty Acres. Sarnoff asked Major Andrew J. White, editor of the magazine *Wireless Age*, to set it up.

White got Harry Walker and J. O. Smith, a couple of radio technicians (there weren't many around in those days) to help him. The three learned that the General Electric Company had just built a transmitter for the U. S. Navy, but hadn't yet delivered it. White managed to borrow it for the fight broadcast.

That was the only thing that came easy. From then on, all White and his associates had was trouble. In his book, *History of Radio*, Gleeson L. Archer tells what happened next.

"Time was short," Archer writes, "so Major White went to the officials of the Lackawanna Railroad and wheedled them into permitting him to suspend an aerial between two of their experimental train wireless towers in Hoboken. The three men carried into a galvanized shack, which served as a dressing room to Pullmen porters, a fearsome collection of radio equipment. The indignant porters threatened the trio with violence, even though the railroad company had given permission to use the shack. Smith slept beside the set in the shack for fear the angry porters might wreck the equipment."

The fight was held on July 2. The night before was a long one for White, Walker, and Smith, who spent most of it testing and retesting the equipment. At 4 A.M., leaving Smith at the shack, the other two went to the arena to set up the microphone at ringside. Their troubles there are described in the book, *This Thing Called Broadcasting:*

"Having surrendered their tickets at the gate [Walker and White] could not leave the enclosure. They had nothing to eat. They sat and smoked and worried. Intermittent showers dampened their clothes and skin. Their spirits were already dampened. When the sun finally rose . . . steam rose from the arena . . . and themselves.

"Finally the arena began to fill, became crowded, the hour arrived and the fight was on. White had not thought how he was going to announce it. He had no time to think, only to worry. At first, he could not start. But being an amateur boxer, he soon became lost in the enthusiasm of the occasion, and keeping his eye glued to the fighters, announced in the ready, clear, natural style that marks the man who knows whereof he speaks."

Actually, White was talking by phone to Smith at the transmitter in Hoboken, and Smith was then rebroadcasting the account over the air. Between rounds, Smith told White over the phone that everything was coming through. In the meantime, Smith himself wasn't exactly having a picnic.

"Standing close to the transmitter, he was partially blind for days afterwards from the glaring tubes," the account continues. "The equipment was not built for continuous service with the power that was being used. It became hotter and hotter. In the middle of the last round, having been on the air more than four hours, one tube exploded. Smith pulled the base from the socket and quickly inserted a new one. After the final signing off he went to the hospital to have the palms of his burned hands bandaged. Before the end of the fight, the transmitter had begun to smoke and shortly after the finish of the program, it resolved itself into a molten mass."

But with all its troubles, the broadcast was a success. Over two hundred thousand people heard the fight.

After that the radio sports parade really got rolling. On August 4, 1921, Station KDKA did the Davis Cup matches, and followed it the next day with the first major league baseball broadcast, through a wire linked from Pittsburgh's Forbes Field to the transmitter.

The first radio station to serve the metropolitan New York area was WJJ, Newark, which opened on October 5, 1921. In its first broadcast it featured World Series bulletins. The series was also the top story in the first network broadcast, a hookup between New York's WJZ and Schenectady's WGY in October of 1922. That was also the year of the first broadcast of a football game direct from the scene, the Princeton-Chicago game over WEAF, New York.

Even in those early days radio turned to sports experts as commentators. Instead of athletes and coaches they used famous sportswriters. The first was Grantland Rice, who did well and often appeared on the air. But the next, Bill McGeehan, sports editor of the New York *Herald* and one of the funniest writers of his generation, hated the job. He was hired to announce the 1923 World Series between the Giants and the Yankees. According to the WEAF program sheets, he quit after the third game. Graham McNamee, a young singer who had worked with McGeehan in the first three games, finished the Series alone.

That launched McNamee on a fabulous career as radio's first glamour boy. His "voice with a smile" became familiar to millions of sports fans all over the country. During the late twenties he broadcast just about every major sports event worth broadcasting. He made history at the 1927 Rose Bowl game between Stanford and Alabama. With KFI, Los Angeles, the originating station, that was the first west-to-east coast-to-coast radio broadcast.

Besides having a great voice, McNamee was smart, a master at creating atmosphere, an artist at ad libbing, and a realistic color man. He and Philip Carlin got together to become the first sports announcing team in radio. Carlin, who later became eastern program manager for N.B.C., was the first top broadcaster without a musical background.

Until he came along, the only announcers who got anywhere were former singers.

In the early days of radio, anyone with a good voice could become a sports announcer. Ted Husing was the first real expert to get behind a mike. Although he eventually logged more time in special events and music pickups than in sports, Husing, in my opinion, was the greatest sportscaster who ever lived.

During the years up to the outbreak of World War II, he was the most versatile and skillful announcer in the business. He had a magnificent voice, beautiful diction, a wide-ranging vocabulary, and a sound knowledge of all the sports he covered. He never tried to broadcast a game cold. He was the first announcer to talk to players, coaches, and experts before going on the air. He never had to fill time with descriptions of the countryside or endless identification of attending celebrities. When he did a sports event, he was all sports, knowledgeable and authoritative.

One of his most significant contributions to modern sportscasting was his judicious use of competent assistants. Nobody had ever had assistants before. Announcers teamed up in pairs to relieve each other on the air, but then didn't see each other from the end of one event to the beginning of the next. Husing hired full-time help. His first assistant was Les Quaily, who later was succeeded by Jimmy Dolan. Both were old friends of Husing and both eventually became top broadcasting executives.

Quaily, who represents the Atlantic Refining Company for N. W. Ayer, is a close associate of mine, since Atlantic is one of the three Red Sox sponsors, along with the Narragansett Brewing Company and the General Cigar Company. He told me Husing took his first lessons in inside football from Knute Rockne, the Notre Dame coach who dominated the game when Husing first began broadcasting.

"Ted had only a fan's knowledge of football," Quaily

said. "He wanted to learn all he could about it. Rockne, always ahead of his time, recognized what radio could do to popularize the college game, so he went out of his way to help. He let Husing attend Notre Dame practice sessions and sit in on locker room talks and discussions, then spent hours explaining and answering questions. Husing learned the business from a master."

Husing had electric spotting boards for instant identification of players on the field, with slots and little bulbs at each position. One of the assistant's jobs was to press buttons under the name of the ballcarrier, the tackler, the passer, the receiver, or anyone else involved in a play, and the proper bulb would light up. All Ted had to do was glance down and everything was right in front of him. With his flair for showmanship, he made a big thing of his boards. He insisted that they be brought up through the crowd covered by a black cloth. For years nobody but Husing and his assistant knew what they were. The system worked well in those days, when only fifteen or twenty men played for each team, but present-day platoon football, with hordes of substitutes streaming in and out, would make Husing's boards obsolete.

Although best known for football, Husing's rowing, tennis, and track and field broadcasts were superb. He studied these sports as carefully as he studied football, preparing for events far in advance so that he would know exactly what he was talking about.

He had a reputation of being temperamental, but I never found him so. When I went to New York in 1946 to broadcast the N.C.A.A. championship basketball game between Oklahoma A. & M. and North Carolina for KOMA, Husing was wonderful to me. My boss, Ken Brown, had asked him to talk to me, and I went to see him in his office at C.B.S. at about two o'clock one afternoon.

"Had breakfast?" he asked.

"This morning," I said.

"Come on down while I have mine," he said.

I sat with him for two hours while he talked about all phases of sports announcing—how to prepare for events, what records to keep, what mistakes to watch for, how to improve my voice, just about everything a man could think of. Then he stood up and asked, "Ever been around the town?"

I shook my head.

"Come on," he said. "I'll show you the place."

For the next three hours, the top sports announcer in the business took a hopeful unknown from the hinterlands on a personally guided tour of Manhattan, complete with a running commentary in one of the nation's most famous voices.

Husing's remarkable career had a tragic ending. Blinded by a brain tumor, he died in obscurity on the West Coast a few years ago. But he left a heritage that will live as long as radio. With his, "Hello, everybody, everywhere," he helped make radio sports exciting and great, and blazed new trails for those of us who followed him.

Some of the other fine sportscasters of those early years of radio were Bill Stern, Bill Slater, Bill Munday, Tom Manning, Sam Taub, and Clem McCarthy. Munday did football in Atlanta, and was famous for his southern drawl and colorful phraseology, such as "craps shooters formation" for the huddle and "land of milk and honey" for the goal line. Manning, "the old redhead," (followed, years later, by another wonderful "old redhead," Red Barber) broadcast baseball in Cleveland in 1925, and shared the World Series microphone with Graham McNamee in 1929. He still has a daily sports show in Cleveland, where I visit with him every summer.

Manning once told me about the first golf broadcast. "We did the National Open at Toledo in 1931 with two bicycles and two stepladders," he said. "Billy Burke and George Von Helm met in the longest playoff in Open history.

I would climb a stepladder at the green, describe the putting, then jump down, get on the bike, and pedal like hell down the fairway to the next green, where the other ladder was set up."

Husing's nearest rival in the thirties was Bill Stern. He made factual mistakes for which he was often criticized, but nobody could match him for dramatic delivery. He had one of the finest voices ever heard on the air. His Friday night sports show over N.B.C., "The Colgate Sports Reel," was undoubtedly the most popular studio sports program in radio history. I once watched him originate the show from Denver in 1944. He spent hours in rehearsal with a Hollywood celebrity guest and a quartet that opened and closed the show and supplied background music for his dramatic stories. He was a master in production.

Slater, who broadcast over Mutual, was a West Point graduate with a brilliant mind. Sports was only one of his specialties, for he could handle any type of radio show. For years he was the host of "Twenty Questions," and he also did a popular daily show out of New York called "Luncheon at Sardi's." He was suddenly forced into retirement in 1950 by a crippling illness.

McCarthy, a lovable, warm-hearted gentleman, was one of the best racing and boxing broadcasters who ever lived. He had a rasping voice, and an exciting delivery which is still widely copied. His career was also ended by illness and long hospitalization. It was a tragic coincidence that three of the greatest announcers of their day, Husing, Slater, and McCarthy, were all prematurely cut down by disabling sicknesses.

After McNamee, Sam Taub was American's favorite fight broadcaster for years. He loved boxing, made an extensive study of it, and set the stage for Don Dunphy and Bill Corum, who followed him. Dunphy, with his accurate, incisive blow-by-blow descriptions, and Corum, with his growling voice giving color and information between rounds, made up the best boxing team broadcasting has ever known.

The earliest baseball announcers were France Laux in St. Louis, Hal Totten, Pat Flanagan and Quin Ryan in Chicago, Arch McDonald in Washington, Rosy Roswell in Pittsburgh, and Fred Hoey in Boston. Red Barber came out of Florida in the thirties to work for the Cincinnati Reds, then owned by Larry MacPhail. When MacPhail went to Brooklyn, Barber went with him to do the Dodgers' games. Now with the Yankees, Red is one of the two oldest major league broadcasters in point of service. The other is Bob Elson of Chicago, who travels with the White Sox. He started with the Cubs in the early thirties. My former mentor, Mel Allen, went to New York from Birmingham as a staff announcer with C.B.S., then joined the Yankees to become a national celebrity. His "How about that!" has become part of the American language.

In recent years, many former athletes have moved into sports broadcasting. Some are good, some fair, some not very promising. The earliest ballplayers to become broadcasters were Jack Graney in Cleveland, Harry Heilmann in Detroit, and Waite Hoyt in Cincinnati. Dizzy Dean, who started broadcasting St. Louis Browns' games, became a standout. He made far more money in radio and television than he ever made as one of baseball's most colorful pitchers.

I sympathize with young sports announcers coming up today, for they must compete with athletes whose names are already well known to American sports followers. I was lucky in starting early enough not to run up against sponsors' preferences for former stars. In a small way, of course, my own sports background helped me. I might not have been able to get into radio in Cheyenne if I hadn't been well known locally as a high school and college basketball player.

I've often been asked if established announcers resent

the influx of ex-stars walking into big broadcasting jobs without any microphone experience. I can't speak for others, but I certainly don't resent it. A former athlete knows his game as no one else does. With intelligence and hard work he can contribute a great deal to a broadcast, provided, of course, he has a passable voice. However, I think he should be teamed up with a professional announcer. The ideal combination is the pro broadcaster and the old pro star.

Television has brought new challenges in one way, made life easier in another. You can't afford to pull a bloop with millions of people watching the same thing you're watching. On the other hand, you have much less describing to do. Some announcers can't shake old radio habits; they talk too much. Television audiences not only don't need this, but resent it. They can see for themselves what's happening. The announcer's job is to fill them in with background material or call attention to highlights—in as few words as possible.

When I work on television, I try to talk to my audience just as I would to a friend watching TV with me. If we were alone and something interesting happened, I'd say, "Look at that!" or "How do you like the way so-and-so runs?" or "That ball's gone!" That's the sort of thing I say on the air. I let the screen tell most of the story.

That's why TV announcing is easier than radio. In radio, the announcer is the only link between the game and the audience. He must describe accurately and succinctly what he sees because the audience can't see it with him. If he does a poor job, he ruins it for everybody because there's no other way the listener can know what's going on. But if a television announcer does a poor job, the viewer can tune him out and still get some enjoyment by just watching.

Some of the earliest telecasts were of sports events—the Columbia-Princeton baseball game, a Dodgers-Reds ball game, the Fordham-Waynesburg football game, all in 1939.

After that everything was quiet until after World War II.

As in the case of radio, television's coming of age was hastened through sports. The first big broadcast was the 1947 World Series between the Dodgers and the Yankees. The Series, sponsored by Ford and Gillette over stations in New York, Philadelphia, Washington, and Schenectady, was sold for sixty-five thousand dollars. It has since become a great national television event, a prized fixture that carries a price tag running into millions.

I was introduced to television while working for the Yankees in the late forties. I couldn't have picked a better time. New York was the center of the booming young industry, nobody knew any more about it than anyone else, and we were all constantly experimenting. I literally grew up with television. I made my mistakes in comparative privacy, for few people owned television sets, which in those early days were almost prohibitively expensive.

Some people thought television would knock radio out of business, but of course it didn't, and I don't think it ever will. There is plenty of room for both, especially in sports. Fans prefer to watch, but will settle for listening if they must. Millions of automobile radios and small transistors help to keep the old medium alive and of prime importance. No aspiring sports announcer can afford to train for television alone. He must be able to handle himself at a radio microphone, too, for radio is bigger now than it was before television.

Every major league ball club uses both media and expects its announcers to be equally proficient at both. The Red Sox televise twice a week and on special occasions. The rest of the time its broadcasts are confined to radio. The men who work with me must be able to shift back and forth at will.

I've been fortunate in the baseball broadcasting partners I've had. It's a long summer and a small booth. There's no room for friction or personality clashes. If broadcasting partners don't get along, they make life miserable for each other, for we not only have to work together, but live and travel together. Fellows like Bob DeLaney, Bob Murphy, Bill Crowley, the late Art Gleeson, and Ned Martin and Mel Parnell, my present partners, have helped make baseball broadcasting a pleasure for me as well as a job. I've been just as fortunate in football, for Paul Christman, with whom I have worked for six years, is one of my closest friends.

We started together on A.B.C., and shifted to N.B.C. with the American Football League, whose games we telecast. When the league made the change at the end of the 1964 season, Commissioner Joe Foss asked Carl Lindemann, N.B.C.'s vice president in charge of sports, to take Paul and me along. Besides A.F.L. games, we also do college football, including Bowl events, for N.B.C.

This change didn't end my connection with A.B.C., which has been close for years and which, I hope, will stay that way. I still host their "American Sportsman's Show," which has been growing each year. This one-hour hunting and fishing program in full color started with four shows a year, went up to eleven, and now is at twenty.

It's a good life I lead, hectic, wonderful, dynamic. The future holds promise of even more excitement, for radio is a teen-ager and television still only a child. Tremendous changes, transformations, and improvements are yet to come.

I hope I'll see them and share in them and, perhaps, contribute something to them.

EPILOGUE

Things move fast in the sports broadcasting world. Since the last chapter of this book was written I have taken on a new challenge, and when the new baseball season opens I shall be handling the play-by-play of the major league "Game of the Week" on N.B.C. television. Instead of being in ten American League cities each summer, I will now be broadcasting from all the major league cities across America. It is with real regret and sadness that I leave the Boston Red Sox and their owner, the marvelous Tom Yawkey, who have been such an important part of my life for the past fifteen years. I think my biggest thrill would be to be able to broadcast the Red Sox in a World Series game.